#ENOUGH

Plays to End Gun Violence

BY

Adelaide Fisher
Eislinn Gracen
Azya Lyons
Debkanya Mitra
Olivia Ridley
Sarah Schecter
& Elizabeth Shannon

Table of Contents

Preface

What art can do is only limited by who we allow to do it. The seven young writers you will meet in #ENOUGH's collection will prove with their surprising, sensitive, soaring plays that theatre's limitless potential is in the hands of the young people. Young people's voices and storytelling power is necessary no matter what subject we are circulating, but certainly when it comes to the grip gun violence has on our nation. We need plays written by the very same citizens who find themselves too often in the crosshairs of a school shooter. We need their voices. We need these voices.

Each play in this collection offers a chance to explore a unique theatrical world, aesthetic, or perspective. Collectively these plays are experimental, fantastical, and then intimate, realistic. All are excellent, exhilarating, and essentially human. Together they are a secret garden of experiences. Come in, explore, stop and smell all the roses, but beware that beautiful things can sting too.

I discovered my love for writing, specifically dramatic writing, when I was the age of all the women in this collection. I recognize their drive, guts, and creativity. I recall the self-doubt and silencing of young voices (particularly young women's voices). I remember the gust of wind I had to summon in myself to take the leap into writing. So I applaud them—Adelaide, Eislinn, Ayza, Debkanya, Olivia, Sarah and Elizabeth—for their artistry and ambition.

I also want to applaud and encourage all of the playwrights around the country who submitted work for #ENOUGH. I can speak for my fellow readers and panelists when I say how moving and inspiring it was to read so many great new works for the stage that braided together art and activism. Theatre is in good hands.

America's flood of gun violence isn't about statistics, but about people. Lives, families, dreams and hopes cut short brutally, unnecessarily, preventably. Gun violence is about voices silenced. Which makes the young voices in this collection all the more potent. They are speaking, dreaming, creating for so many who can't.

— Lauren M. Gunderson, March 2, 2021

Lauren is a two-time winner of the ATCA/Steinberg new play Award and has topped a list of the most-produced playwrights in America.

Note on Producing All Seven Plays Together

Hashtag Enough

The hashtag (#) of #ENOUGH is part of the title and is spoken out loud. For example, in the Prologue the line "In 2020, #ENOUGH called on teen writers..." should be said "In 2020, Hashtag ENOUGH called on teen writers..."

Performance Order

If you produce all seven plays together for an evening of theatre, the order in which the plays have been published in this anthology is also the order that they should be presented in your production, with the Prologue and Epilogue available to you to bookend the plays.

Assigning Speakers for Prologue and Epilogue

Both the Prologue and Epilogue can be arranged among your performers however you see fit. They can be read by an ensemble or by a single speaker. The text could even be projected or pre-recorded. It's up to you.

In the Epilogue, the final "ENOUGH" can be said simultaneously by your cast, repeated until all members of your cast have said it, or any number of permutations.

Required Program Credit

The digital premiere of #ENOUGH: Plays to End Gun Violence was co-produced by #ENOUGH: Plays to End Gun Violence (Michael Cotey, Producer) and Alliance Theatre, Arizona Theatre Company, Berkeley Repertory Theatre, Goodman Theatre, Orlando Repertory Theatre, and South Coast Repertory.

"This is *precisely* the time when artists go to work. There is no time for despair, no place for self-pity, no need for silence, no room for fear. We speak, we write, we do language. That is how civilizations heal."

— Toni Morrison

Prologue

More than 200 Americans are shot and wounded every day.

100 more Americans are killed every day with guns.

8 of those killed everyday are children and teens.

In 2020, #ENOUGH called on teen writers to channel their fear and frustration,

their anxiety and anger,

and, yes, their hope

into ten-minute plays that tackle the issue of gun violence.

This is what they had to say.

LOADED LANGUAGE
by Elizabeth Shannon

Cast of Characters

KIERSA, F, a student at Trojan High School.

AMIRA, F, a student at Trojan High School.

JJ, F, a student at Trojan High School.

LOGAN, M, a student at Trojan High School.

WILL, M, a student at Trojan High School.

Casting Note

Genders of all the characters can be flexible and pronouns can be adjusted to fit your actors. Please ensure that casting is diverse. At least one person in the cast should be BIPOC.

Setting

Scene One and Three: Each character is in their own space. Some can be sitting, others standing; although they speak to the audience, they may have previous action that we can see. As the scene progresses, they may leave where they were sitting/standing and become more connected.

Scene Two: A school classroom, right before the bell rings. Again, the set can be minimal, as long as it gives some hint of a classroom.

Production Note

"/" indicates an overlap in dialogue. When this is seen in someone's line, it cues the person with the next line to start speaking.

Author's Note

I have written plays before, but never seemed it necessary to include a note. This one, however, is different. In both scenes, all of the experiences of these characters are things I have thought, said, or had happen to me.

Speaking specifically to the second scene, an event very similar to what I've written happened to me my sophomore year of high school, in my third block biology class. Although some details have been changed, the events are still real. In short, I overheard questionable talk of a shooting, without context.

When I saw the prompt about writing about the impact of gun violence, this experience was the first thing I thought of, and I knew immediately I had to write it. Obviously it strikes a personal chord with me, but it also does with people across the nation. Even if we have not been the victim of a shooting, we have had close calls. We have heard a noise in a crowd and ran, we have picked out exits in a crowded building. As I write this, I am reminded of the video of a vehicle backfiring in Times Square, and thousands of people running for shelter, thinking that the horrific was finally happening to them. I wanted to show how the anxiety of shootings is present everywhere, even when a shooting doesn't occur.

Lastly, I had a few of my friends proofread the script for me. Without realizing it, I asked one of my friends who was involved in the biology incident to read it. She texted me afterwards and asked if it was based on what she thought it was based on, and told me how it brought back all of her feelings about that day. In the actual event, we went to our fourth block classes and shortly after a member of administration pulled us out to tell us that everything was all right. I remember sitting in my fourth block, completely numb. We were all so scared. We still are.

Elizabeth Shannon

Acknowledgments

Loaded Language was awarded a winner of the 2020 #ENOUGH: Plays to End Gun Violence competition and received further development with #ENOUGH: Plays to End Gun Violence (Michael Cotey, Producer). It was produced as part of #ENOUGH's Nationwide Reading and had its digital premiere produced by South Coast Repertory (Costa Mesa, CA) for Broadway on Demand on December 14, 2020. It was directed by Anna Jennings; the assistant director was Olivia Drury. The play was sponsored by Jeanne Duncan. The cast was as follows:

KIERSA . . . . Halia Lindauer
AMIRA . . . . Katie Lee
JJ. . . . . Josina Montes
LOGAN. . . . . Vincent Logan
WILL . . . . Nick Trafton

Required Program Credit

The digital premiere of *Loaded Language* was co-produced by #ENOUGH: Plays to End Gun Violence (Michael Cotey, Producer) and South Coast Repertory (Costa Mesa, CA) for Broadway on Demand.

LOADED LANGUAGE
by Elizabeth Shannon

Scene One

(A blank stage, except for KIERSA, AMIRA, JJ, LOGAN, AND WILL, *who are sitting/standing. Lights rise on each character when they speak their first line.)*

KIERSA. Before last year, my school basically let anyone in the front door. I mean, they still do, but they installed these "security doors" recently, so someone entering has to go through the front office before entering the rest of the school.

AMIRA. We all thought it was stupid. It made getting to class much harder—

JJ. And it wasn't like they were gonna stop anyone.

LOGAN. Our school has a lot of doors. Doors by the theatre, doors by the gym . . . Some kids prop them open so they can sneak out of school and come back later.

AMIRA. A shooter could enter from any number of those doors, totally undetected.

WILL. And even if the "security doors" did stop them from going immediately into the hallway, they could just . . . shoot the people in the front office and then walk through.

KIERSA. The doors are pointless.

AMIRA. Not to mention, a lot of times, school shooters are students. They just walk in with everyone else at the beginning of the day, no questions asked.

LOGAN. It would be *so easy*— I mean, don't call the cops, I'm not a shooter, but I could think of, like, a million ways to sneak a weapon in.

KIERSA. My teacher told me a story about this one kid who made a threat, and the police and principal showed up in my teacher's classroom in bulletproof vests first block to take him out of school.

JJ. We don't have lunch periods here, we just have one hour of free time.

AMIRA. And there isn't enough space in the cafeteria, so people basically just eat wherever.

LOGAN. It's kinda gross, actually.

AMIRA. My friends sit at the front of the school, but I never stay there too long. The reason why is simple: if a shooter was gonna come in—and lunch would be the perfect time to—we'd be the first ones dead.

WILL. I pick what classes I take partly based on where the rooms are located.

JJ. The choir room is connected to the stage. I take a lot of choir classes, 'cause, well ... if someone comes in, there are a million places I could hide. I know them all. There's the catwalk, the dressing rooms, the backstage bathrooms no one knows about, and these giant prop and costume rooms with big steel doors.

KIERSA. The choir room even has its own exit out of the building, right near the parking lot where I park my car.

JJ. You have the best chance of survival in that room.

KIERSA. So I'm in it as much as possible.

AMIRA. One day, my dad was driving me to school. He was listening to a report about a school shooting that had happened the day before. Why didn't he turn it off? I was sitting there, *on my way to school.*

KIERSA. My mom told me once how she worries every time she drops me off. What if she doesn't see me again? Then she told me that she realized that her worrying probably doesn't even compare to how I feel walking into school everyday. She was right.

LOGAN. I say goodbye to my parents, and it always crosses my mind that I might not see them again. I just ... shove that thought away.

WILL. I've planned what my last text will say, in case something happens.

JJ. I was a fourth grader when Sandy Hook happened. That could have been me.

WILL. I was a freshman when Parkland happened. A lot of the kids killed there were my age.

ALL. That could have been me.

Scene Two

(Sudden shift. Bright lights, reminiscent of the fluorescent school lighting, rise on a school classroom, a few minutes before class lets out. JJ, KIERSA, and AMIRA are standing in a group, talking, although KIERSA is looking at her phone and not really paying attention. WILL and LOGAN are talking close by.)

JJ. So on Saturday, I'm going to the movies, then I have work on Sunday.

AMIRA. Oh, damn, I was gonna ask if we could hang out.

JJ. Could we on Monday?

(Lights shift to LOGAN and WILL. JJ and AMIRA continue to speak, but more quietly. These two conversations are going on at the same time, though the focus is more on LOGAN and WILL.)

LOGAN. Did you hear that Chad and Ella broke up?

AMIRA. Monday / I have swim.

WILL. No shit!

LOGAN. Yeah. Apparently Chad is, like, super pissed at Ella.

JJ. Well, I'm busy / Tuesday . . .

WILL. Why?

LOGAN. I don't know . . . / but if I were Ella, I wouldn't have messed with Chad. You know he has, like, anger issues, or some shit, right? I bet he's gonna shoot this place / up.

AMIRA. Wednesday? I'm free then.

JJ. Let me check.

(JJ pulls out her phone. KIERSA overhears LOGAN's line, and registers the statement. She continues to listen.)

WILL. No way.

LOGAN. I think so. And I know his dad keeps guns in their house— I went over once and Chad showed them to me—so he totally could do it. He and Ella have the same fourth block, so my money is on him doing it / then.

JJ. Yeah, I think / Wednesday works.

WILL. Oh, shit, that's in, like, 10 minutes.

(KIERSA leans forward, staring at JJ and AMIRA.)

JJ. Yeah?

KIERSA. Did you hear them?

AMIRA. Who?

KIERSA. Logan and Will.

AMIRA. . . . No, what did they say?

KIERSA. Something, about, um, Chad—

JJ. And Ella? Yeah, they broke up.

KIERSA. No, he was talking about Chad . . . shooting this place up.

JJ. Oh.

AMIRA. What?

JJ. Are you sure that's what he said? That doesn't seem like Chad.

KIERSA. Well, I—I overheard it, and they weren't talking super loud. I mean, I really just heard shooting, I could've misheard . . .

AMIRA. It's probably just that, or they were joking around. You know Logan, he's an asshole.

KIERSA. *(Trying to be convinced:)* Yeah.

> *(Everyone sits quietly for a moment, then* JJ *and* AMIRA *start talking again.)*

JJ. Are you going to the game on Friday?

AMIRA. I was thinking about it

JJ. You should ask Carlos to go with you!

AMIRA. Oh my God, he would never say yes—

KIERSA. Should we tell Ms. Alby?

JJ. Tell her what?

KIERSA. What I heard.

AMIRA. Um, I mean, if you think you heard it correctly . . .

> *(KIERSA's hand starts shaking a bit, and she stares directly at one spot in front of her.)*

JJ. *Did* you hear correctly? You're kinda freaking me out—

AMIRA. Are you okay, Kiersa? You look kinda . . .

KIERSA. What if Chad is planning that? What if he has a gun? I have to cross the main hallway to get to my next class, he could be there . . .

AMIRA. I'm sure he won't be.

(KIERSA *is trying to steady her breath.*)

JJ. Here, how about we tell Alby, like you said. Just so you have some peace of mind. I'm sure it's nothing, but you don't look too good.

(JJ *gives* AMIRA *a look, silently asking for support.*)

AMIRA. Yeah. Look, Alby is right over there. Let's go, okay?

KIERSA. I— I don't want to.

(JJ *and* AMIRA *exchange a look.*)

AMIRA. I'll go. She might ask to talk to you though.

KIERSA. Just, just tell her—

JJ. I'm sure it'll be fine. We'll wait here.

(AMIRA *turns to walk offstage.*)

KIERSA. Thanks, Amira.

(AMIRA *looks at her and nods.*)

AMIRA. No problem.

(AMIRA *exits.* JJ *and* KIERSA *sit together,* KIERSA *wringing her hands. After a moment:)*

JJ. You really think you heard that?

KIERSA. *(Robotic:)* I don't know.

JJ. Well, um. I'm sure everything will be okay. That kinda stuff doesn't happen here.

KIERSA. Not yet.

JJ. You know Logan and Will. They always say stupid shit.

(KIERSA *looks at* JJ.)

JJ. Don't . . . don't get me wrong, I believe you. Just trying to . . .

KIERSA. Yeah. Thanks.

(JJ *eyes* LOGAN *and* WILL *warily.* AMIRA *enters from the same place she exited, crossing to* JJ *and* KIERSA.)

AMIRA. *(Hushed:)* I told her.

JJ. And?

AMIRA. She's calling admin.

(KIERSA *takes a deep breath and sighs.*)

AMIRA. What did you expect?

KIERSA. I don't know. I mean, this. I figured she'd call. But still.

AMIRA. *(Not wanting to make things worse:)* . . . And she said she'd talk to Logan and Will.

(KIERSA *gives* JJ *and* AMIRA *a wide-eyed look.*)

KIERSA. What if I heard wrong? Oh God, Logan is gonna know it was me. He's gonna tell everyone I'm a pussy. Shit . . .

AMIRA. Hey. Better safe than sorry.

JJ. Are you okay, Kiersa?

KIERSA. *(Nodding:)* It was just, just . . . my anxiety. You know. Being trapped in a room with no doors and hearing . . . *that* . . . not super great.

(*She breathes deeply.*)

AMIRA. Yeah, I figured. I mean, I feel the same way.

JJ. Like, like a panic attack?

KIERSA. I guess. Yeah.

(KIERSA, JJ, *and* AMIRA *glance at* LOGAN *and* WILL, *then turn into a small huddle-like group. Lights fade on* WILL *and* LOGAN.)

KIERSA. You think they'll be pulled out of class?

AMIRA. *(Shrugging:)* Maybe. Probably in fourth period.

JJ. *(Checking her phone:)* I mean, there's only two minutes left of class. You know the bells are automatic, and admin won't make an announcement.

AMIRA. *(Lightheartedly:)* Yeah, and the intercoms don't even work, you can't even hear them in half of the classrooms. This school seriously is a piece of shit.

KIERSA. *(With a small laugh:)* Yeah.

(*Lights rise back up on* LOGAN *and* WILL.)

LOGAN. *(To* WILL, *annoyed:)* Who snitched?

WILL. For real. Why can't anyone take a joke . . .

(KIERSA *looks at* JJ *and* AMIRA.)

JJ. *(Whispering:)* They don't know it's you.

KIERSA. They could've seen you talking with Alby—

AMIRA. Who cares? They won't get in trouble, anyways. Everything's good. Just . . . go to fourth block and try to forget about it.

KIERSA. It didn't happen. We're fine.

JJ. Exactly. We're fine—nothing happened, and it's not going to.

AMIRA. Not today, at least.

(KIERSA takes a deep breath and wrings her hands. AMIRA and JJ pat her on the shoulder/give her a hug/lean on her, etc. The bell rings, and AMIRA, JJ, and KIERSA walk out, KIERSA still slightly shaky.)

Scene Three

(A gradual shift, not as sudden as the previous scene change. Lights rise back on the chorus setting we saw in the first scene.)

JJ. We all think it. No one ever thinks "that won't happen".

LOGAN. Teachers have close-doored discussions with us about it.

WILL. Sometimes you'll be in class and you'll hear a—

ALL. POP—

WILL. From down the hall.

JJ. The entire class freezes.

AMIRA. We all look at each other and have this moment of—

ALL. Holy shit. It's happening.

KIERSA. And it'll just be a balloon or a science class doing an experiment or something, but . . .

JJ. You feel it in your chest. That fear, that fear that your life is about to end.

LOGAN. A teacher told me once that I don't have to worry about my school being shot up. Her reasoning? I go to an inner city school. She said that most schools with shooters are rich, predominantly white schools. So *I'll* be fine—but the kids at rich schools? They might not be.

JJ. When I was a freshman, one of my best friends in a neighboring school told me someone was planning on shooting up his school at one o'clock. The school knew about the threat, but all the kids were still there. I made my friend text me every five minutes that he was safe.

AMIRA. My friends will text me: don't go to school tomorrow. This kid posted that he's gonna bring a gun.

JJ. Every high school in my county, hell, probably my state, has had a shooter threat—and most have had more than one.

LOGAN. But it's not just schools. It's concerts—

JJ. Movies—

AMIRA. Festivals—

WILL. Farmer's markets—

ANY WHITE STUDENT. And I don't even have to worry about being killed by a police officer while walking down the street.

ANY STUDENT OF COLOR. I could be killed for jogging in my neighborhood, or walking my dog after dark.

KIERSA. This isn't a hypothetical.

(The students stand in a line.)

ALL. This is now.

(BLACKOUT.)

End of Play

MALCOLM
by Debkanya Mitra

Cast of Characters

SISTER, the woman who Malcolm grew up with.

BANDMATE, a close friend of Malcolm.

COLLEGE FRIEND, a confident lawyer on this case. A person of color.

DRIVER, the person who gave Malcolm his last ride.

Acknowledgments

Malcolm was awarded a winner of the 2020 #ENOUGH: Plays to End Gun Violence competition and received further development with #ENOUGH: Plays to End Gun Violence (Michael Cotey, Producer). It was produced as part of #ENOUGH's Nationwide Reading and had its digital premiere produced by Arizona Theatre Company for Broadway on Demand on December 14, 2020. It was directed by Nickole Custodio; the production manager was Roark Polzin; costume designs by Roark Polzin and Zoie Staats; lighting design by Isabella Beres; sound design by Leander Rios; sound editor by Olivia Santellenes; animation by Rain Bousquet; the assistant director was Zoie Staats. The play was sponsored by Fred Kingsley. The cast was as follows:

COLLEGE FRIEND.................... Faith Santos
BANDMATE .... Preston Campbell
DRIVER......................... Lauren Youngstedt
SISTER................................. Petra Polzin

Required Program Credit

The digital premiere of *Malcolm* was co-produced by #ENOUGH: Plays to End Gun Violence (Michael Cotey, Producer) and Arizona Theatre Company for Broadway on Demand.

MALCOLM
by Debkanya Mitra

(SISTER, BANDMATE, COLLEGE FRIEND, *and* DRIVER *enter.*)

COLLEGE FRIEND. He said his name was Malcolm.
I said—"like Malcolm X?"
He said he didn't believe in violence

BANDMATE. He had a soulful voice
played a mean guitar too

We played a diner in Atlanta and the guy who owned it called him
a couple different slurs
they almost fought but I held him back said "he deserves a punch
but don't do it"

Next day he said he needed to go home

COLLEGE FRIEND. "Where's home?" I asked
He said Saponi Falls

DRIVER. Most people don't take hitchhikers anymore.
They're worried. I'm not.

I picked him up down in Atlanta.
I dropped him off in Saponi Falls.

SISTER. We grew up there. Maryland. A suburb of DC. Nothing big
ever happened in Saponi Falls. People there are liberal—I think it
could be one of the most liberal places in the US outside California.
Everyone was surprised when they . . . heard the news. Everyone
trusted the police.

It wasn't supposed to happen to him.
It wasn't supposed to happen here.

But there's a video—and you can see it—and you can hear each word
the police said—and you can hear my brother's loud breath—trying
to cling to life.

BANDMATE. I told him not to leave Atlanta
But he had to leave

He had something to tell his sister

27

SISTER. He texted me telling me that he had something important to say. And he kept saying sorry. "Sorry, sorry, sorry." He said, "I should've told you earlier but I didn't."

I was excited that he was coming home. He hadn't been back for a while. We all thought that he was mad at us or something. But he's not like that. He's quiet, observant—

COLLEGE FRIEND. introspective—

SISTER. He's not the kind of guy that complains or gets angry. Ever. He just notices things. When we were younger he noticed the things that I missed.

Once we were driving past a Black Lives Matter protest in the neighborhood. And he told me "isn't it ironic? there isn't a single black person there."

SISTER. It must have been hard for him to grow up in Saponi Falls. Our parents adopted him. I don't know the details. Malcolm never asked.

COLLEGE FRIEND. He was dead-set on learning more about his biological parents
when I met him in college—I was studying African American studies with a minor in statistics, he was studying classical music

BANDMATE. I asked him why he wanted to do folk
and he shrugged

DRIVER. And after he said that he was silent.
He was silent through the Carolinas and through Virginia.
But somehow we understood each other.

BANDMATE. I didn't ask him any more
I get it—
there's something about the music that makes
the pain of a dead end job
a dead end life melt away

COLLEGE FRIEND. Well we did it
We went through databases of internet records
and phone books and we found them—

He was born in Brooklyn
His father died in jail
His mother died having him

When we left college he went to Brooklyn
I went to law school and became a civil rights lawyer

SISTER. It wasn't supposed to happen here.
It wasn't supposed to happen to him.

COLLEGE FRIEND. Malcolm's case is the most important,
most personal one I've ever worked on
it keeps me up at night

Brooklyn taught him that his great grandparents were sharecroppers
on a Georgia plantation
He said he had to go

SISTER. I couldn't understand why he kept moving. But he said he
was fine. He said that he'd tell me—and he sent me postcards from
Atlanta. It's a big city. He said that there were a lot of opportunities.
Teaching guitar and with his band.

COLLEGE FRIEND. I wonder what he saw in Georgia
we drifted apart

SISTER. Somehow he drifted away from all of us, and into music
instead.

BANDMATE. We played clubs and weddings and birthday parties
We played parks and restaurants

We played a diner
and he realized he was done

COLLEGE FRIEND. I think he finally found his anger

BANDMATE. He was deflated.

DRIVER. He was tired when he stepped into my car.
He carried a guitar case.

BANDMATE. I asked him if he was going to come back to Atlanta.
But he was quiet.

COLLEGE FRIEND. I don't like how quiet he gets sometimes
like he's celebrating his own funeral—

I don't know very much about the Saponi
but there was a paragraph on it in one of the textbooks

their language incorporates words of African origin
because the Saponi were one of the tribes that were known
for sheltering runaway slaves

and sometimes, swimming in this ocean of oppression
where justice seems to be what's in shackles
I wonder why.

SISTER. He never came home.

BANDMATE. I've got words for the officer who murdered my bandmate.

SISTER. We held a vigil and people came from everywhere.

BANDMATE. To the man who murdered my bandmate—

you took away my best friend
you took away a man that heals other men
with music—
and you took away his life because of your hatred

DRIVER. We had gotten into the city, Saponi Falls
and night had fallen
I stopped at the gas station near the park
He thanked me and left—into the night—
when I came back from the gas station, before getting into my car
I saw him
walking in the park, whistling

He looked happy and calm—peaceful—
and suddenly there was a fury of activity

Things moved so fast
an officer walked past and I pulled out my camera
the details are fuzzy—but you can see it—hear it—

COLLEGE FRIEND. You can see the way the officer
violates Malcolm's body

BANDMATE. You can hear Malcolm's loud heart

DRIVER. The officer pinned him down
to the concrete footpath of the park.

And a shot rang out.

End of Play

MS. MARTIN'S MALAISE
by Adelaide Fisher

Cast of Characters

MS. MARTIN. A young high school English teacher, stressed, wants the best for everyone.

MARIA. High school student, leader in student government, tries to do what's right, a rule follower.

OSCAR. High school student, regarded as nice by others, cares a lot about his family.

FATE #1. Overly cheerful, speaks in facts, figures, headlines, and messages.

FATE #2. Considers herself to be an optimist, very anxious, overthinker.

FATE #3. Considers themself to be a realist, is actually very negative, knows Ms. Martin's vulnerabilities very personally.

Settings

High school cafeteria
Ms. Martin's classroom
High school courtyard/hallway
Principal's office

Production Note

A note on language: This piece contains a few instances of brief strong language. For those who do not wish to use such language, substitutions have been provided in italicized brackets next to the original text.

Acknowledgments

Ms. Martin's Malaise was awarded a winner of the 2020 #ENOUGH: Plays to End Gun Violence competition and received further development with #ENOUGH: Plays to End Gun Violence (Michael Cotey, Producer). It was produced as part of #ENOUGH's Nationwide Reading and had its digital premiere produced by Orlando Repertory Theatre for Broadway on Demand on December 14, 2020. It was directed by Nathan Tanner Stout; lighting design by Kyle Wiehe. The play was sponsored by John Weidman. The cast was as follows:

> MS. MARTIN . . . . Alaina Jayne Antrim
> OSCAR . . . . David Buitrago-Forero
> MARIA . . . . .Hila Benghiat
> FATE 1 . . . . Cole Higginbotham
> FATE 2 . . . . .Kira Humphrey
> FATE 3 . . . . .Sam Gooden

Required Program Credit

The digital premiere of *Ms. Martin's Malaise* was co-produced by #ENOUGH: Plays to End Gun Violence (Michael Cotey, Producer) and Orlando Repertory Theatre for Broadway on Demand.

MS. MARTIN'S MALAISE
by Adelaide Fisher

Scene 1

(MS. MARTIN *is on cafeteria monitoring duty, drinking an iced coffee,* THE FATES *behind her. Off to the side* MARIA *has a balloon-popping fundraiser set up.* FATE #2 *and* FATE #3 *always address one another when speaking, while* FATE #1 *stares straight out, addressing the audience in the chipper tone of an overexcited newscaster, standing perfectly still and smiling when not speaking. Before each of her lines there should be a ping, like the notification you might hear from an iPhone, and as she is saying them* MS. MARTIN *should check her phone and react to them. All three are dressed the same as* MS. MARTIN, *but in a grayscale version of her outfit.* MS. MARTIN *should react to what* THE FATES *are saying, but should never look at them or address them directly.* THE FATES, *however, can all hear one another.)*

FATE #2. Are there too many kids in here?

FATE #1. Recommended headline: Survey finds 8% of public schools have enrollment that exceeds their permanent capacity by more than 25%.

FATE #2. I feel like there's way too many kids in here.

(MS. MARTIN *starts trying to count the amount of kids in the cafeteria.* FATE #3 *starts nonchalantly sipping an iced coffee, and should continue to do so throughout the scene.)*

FATE #3. *(With a hint of sarcasm:)* I actually think there's less kids in here than normal.

FATE #1. Recommended article: Skipping School: Time Out Adds Up!

FATE #3. Remember all those missing assignments we've been putting in?

FATE #2. No, there's definitely more, do you feel how hot it is in here? Is the air conditioner broken?

(MS. MARTIN *starts fanning herself.)*

FATE #1. Continue Reading: New Research Quantifies The Impact of Extreme Heat on Learning.

FATE #2. What would we do if something happened with this many kids in here? How would they all get out?

FATE #3. They wouldn't.

(OSCAR *enters and goes over to* MARIA.)

OSCAR. Hey, Maria. What's all this?

MARIA. Fundraiser for Student Government. It's a dollar to pop a balloon, and you could win a prize. Want to try?

OSCAR. Sure!

(*He hands her a dollar and she pops one of the balloons.* MS. MARTIN *jumps.* FATE #2 *hits the floor like a bomb is going off.*)

FATE #2. Oh my god, it's literally happening right now. Everyone needs to evacuate, OK, let's go!

FATE #3. That was a balloon popping, idiot. How would you even get everyone's attention?

(*The bell rings, and* MARIA *picks up her poster board with the balloons on it to reveal a laptop and exits.* OSCAR *exits, crossing in front of* MS. MARTIN.)

MS. MARTIN. Hi, Oscar!

OSCAR. Hi Ms. Martin. See you fourth period.

(OSCAR *starts to exit.*)

MS. MARTIN. Oh, hang on a minute. I noticed you haven't been turning in your reading questions on *The Odyssey* the past couple weeks, is there any reason why?

OSCAR. (*Awkwardly:*) Uh, I was going to get caught up this weekend, but I was . . . busy.

MS. MARTIN. Oh . . . ok. Well, if anything is going on you know you can tell me. Um, just try to get caught up, we have a discussion this Friday and you usually have really good input.

(*The minute bell rings and* OSCAR *gives her an uncomfortable nod and smile before leaving.*)

FATE #3. (*Mocking:*) 'If anything is going on you know you can tell me' I can't believe we're really talking like that.

FATE #2. *The Odyssey* . . . I love that book.

FATE #3. You would.

FATE #2. I hope they're enjoying it.

(MS. MARTIN *goes over to the table where the balloons were and sits down in front of the laptop. She is now at her desk in her classroom. She takes off her walkie-talkie and sets it on the table next to her.* THE FATES *gather back around her as she starts working.)*

FATE #2. That was way too close back there.

FATE #3. That was, quite literally, nothing. Why are you so tense all the time?

FATE #2. I'm not *tense.* And at least I had a plan, what were you going to do?

FATE #3. Oh yeah, great plan, "ooh oh no everybody get out." I *know* what to do. We've had how many lockdown drills this year?

FATE #1. Recommended Article: Lockdown Drills: An American Quirk Out of Control.

FATE #2. We've never done one in the cafeteria!

FATE #3. That's because they're completely pointless.

FATE #1. Continue Watching: Tonight we go inside a company that profits off of staging realistic shooter drills—

FATE #2. No they're not!

FATE #1. —a small part of the 2.7 billion dollar school security industry.

FATE #2. They prepare students for the worst!

FATE #3. Maybe. But at what cost?

FATE #1. Message from: Sarah. This is what I've been trying to tell Francis for ages. Saw you jump in the cafeteria by the way, lol. Link: Experts Worry Active Shooter Drills In Schools Could Be Traumatic For Students

> *(The walkie-talkie crackles to life with someone yelling unintelligibly over it, making* MS. MARTIN *and* FATE #2 *jump again.)*

FATE #3. See, look at you, you're a constant wreck. For what?

FATE #2. I just like to be prepared.

FATE #3. For the inevitable, you mean.

FATE #2. No! It's not like that! Don't say that!

> (FATE #2 *and* #3 *continue arguing silently for a beat as* MS. MARTIN *works, looking more and more weary. They switch back on.)*

FATE #2. Why do you have to be such a pessimist all the time!

FATE #3. I'm not a pessimist. I'm a realist.

(MS. MARTIN *sits back down at her desk and sighs as the bell rings.*)

FATE #1. Recommended Reading: Pessimists are 35% more likely to suffer from a heart attack or stroke than optimists, according to a recent meta-analysis of data from—

FATE #2. See! All of your negativity is killing you!

FATE #3. You're not an optimist either.

FATE #2. Yes, I am!

FATE #3. Then why do you worry about everything all the time?

(*All of a sudden,* MARIA *bursts into the classroom, very upset.*)

MARIA. Ms. Martin, I need to tell you something.

MS. MARTIN. What is it, Maria?

(FATE #2 *looks at* FATE #3 *nervously, and she rolls her eyes.*)

MARIA. Do you promise you'll believe me?

MS. MARTIN. Of course. What's going on?

MARIA. Well, last period I was in art class with Oscar and—

FATE #3. Spit it out already!

FATE #2. Shh!

MARIA. He has a gun with him. In his backpack. I saw it.

(FATE #2 *gasps,* FATE #3 *chokes on her coffee.*)

MARIA. And I know you have him next period and I—

MS. MARTIN. Ok. Thank you for telling me, Maria. Go back to class for right now, please. I promise I'll take care of this immediately.

(MARIA *leaves and* MS. MARTIN *stands still, frozen with fear and uncertainty.* FATE #3 *and* FATE #2 *start arguing again, overlapping and cutting one another off.*)

FATE #2. We don't have to tell anyone.

FATE #3. We should just confront him—

FATE #1. Message From: Parson County Library. Overdue book notice: 10 Ways to Make a Confrontation Work for You!

FATE #2. He's such a good kid.

FATE #3. We have to *do* something—

FATE #2. What am I saying? We can't get in trouble for this.

FATE #3. What do we do? You're the one who's supposed to be ready for this!

FATE #1. 10 people liked your comment: "when I think about dealing with a school shooting, the word 'unprepared' comes to mind."

FATE #2. Oh my god, didn't we just email him saying we were going to have to have a conference with his parents if he didn't get caught up on the reading? What if we pissed him off?

FATE #3. This is *not* about us. Stop being so self-centered and *focus*. What do we do?

FATE #2. I—I don't know. I'm scared.

FATE #2 AND FATE #3. Why is this happening?

(The bell rings, snapping everyone out of it. MS. MARTIN starts to get up, but hesitates.)

FATE #1. Message from: Quotey. Quote of the day: "Thinking will not overcome fear, but action will." —W. Clements Stone.

(MS. MARTIN nods, ready now. She picks up her walkie-talkie and moves back into the courtyard, THE FATES following her. OSCAR walks by and sees MS. MARTIN staring at him.)

OSCAR. Um, hi Ms. Martin. Everything OK?

FATE #3. Grab him!

FATE #2. No!

(OSCAR gives MS. MARTIN an awkward half-smile, but then realizes what she knows. There is one, terrible beat before he starts to run and MS. MARTIN grabs his backpack. Blackout.)

Scene Two

(Lights up on a similar desk to Ms. Martin's, differing only in the fact that it belongs to the principal. OSCAR is sitting on one side of it, and MS. MARTIN is taking a seat on the other. THE FATES are already in place, behind MS. MARTIN.)

MS. MARTIN. Ms. Francis said you were begging to talk to me before your parents got here? Why?

OSCAR. Because I like your class. And I probably won't be coming back to it. And I like you, and I didn't want to leave with you thinking I was some troubled, burnout, school shooter.

FATE #3. Isn't that . . . exactly what he is?

OSCAR. I want you to know the truth.

FATE #2. Is this going to get us in trouble?

MS. MARTIN. You did tell the truth to Ms. Francis right?

OSCAR. Yes, and the police. And soon my parents. Which defeats the whole purpose of—

FATE #3. What is he rambling about?

MS. MARTIN. Oscar, just start at the beginning. I'm listening, OK?

OSCAR. OK. I guess, well, I'm not blaming him but this is all really because of my brother.

MS. MARTIN. Your brother? I don't follow.

(OSCAR *gathers his thoughts for a moment, trying to figure out where to start.*)

FATE #3. Why do you think he did it?

FATE #2. I don't know.

FATE #3. I bet he was getting bullied.

FATE #1. Recommended from the headlines: New study shows about 20% of students aged 12-18 have experienced bullying.

FATE #3. Or on drugs.

FATE #2. I said I don't know. *Please* shut up.

FATE #3. Jesus, *[Fine]* OK. Stop taking everything so seriously.

MS. MARTIN. *(Soft, yet focused:)* Can you explain a bit more? Please?

OSCAR. My brother . . . hangs out with the wrong crowd here. Sometimes him and his best friend get into big fights. I knew they were arguing recently and I heard my brother say to his other friend that he was going to finally do something . . . big, finally shut him up. And sometimes when my brother's mad he does things he wouldn't normally do, he gets himself in trouble. But he's *not* a bad person, usually, he can be really nice. And I—

(OSCAR's *voice starts to falter more.*)

I walked in on him in my parents' room. He was holding my dad's gun and he jumped when I asked him what he was doing, and I just— I just got really scared of what he was going to do. So I decided to hide it and I was pretty sure he wasn't going to go in my backpack so I put it there and I was so anxious the whole weekend that he was going to ask me where it went that I forgot to do the reading—

(MS. MARTIN *cringes a little at this.*)

(OSCAR *is letting everything out in a rush now, starting to cry.*)

OSCAR. But then the next day it was Monday morning and I was late and in a rush and I forgot to take it out and then when I got to school and saw it in there I freaked out and then—

MS. MARTIN. Oscar, why didn't you tell someone what was going on?

FATE #3. "Someone"? I think you mean "me." And you know why.

OSCAR. I was scared. And I was worried that you might be mad at me for not doing my work and you wouldn't listen to me. And I didn't want my brother to get in trouble. I want him to be able to graduate, and get a job, and turn his life around.

FATE #3. Ugh, Sarah had his brother last year, didn't she. What'd she call him? A little shit? *[A piece of work?]*

FATE #2. Poor kid, what about *him?*

FATE #3. If we knew about his brother, how did we not know about this?

FATE #1. Two missed calls from: Mom. Message from: Mom. I just got your voicemail, are you OK?

FATE #2. (*To* FATE #3, *still irritated with them:*) How would we have known?

MS. MARTIN. It's sweet that you care so much about your brother, Oscar, but what about you? You're so sm—

OSCAR. (*Trying to hold back tears:*) I know, OK? I'm sorry. I get it, I let everyone down. You all thought I was "different from him."

(MS. MARTIN *looks away, feeling guilty.* OSCAR *passes her a book he's been holding in his lap.*)

OSCAR. The police tried to take this as evidence but I didn't want to steal it from you. And they decided it wasn't actually important, I guess it's no marked up *Catcher in the Rye.*

(*He laughs weakly at this.* MS. MARTIN *picks up the book.*)

FATE #2. *The Odyssey.*

OSCAR. Sorry I never got to finish it. I actually really like it.

MS. MARTIN. Keep it. I still want to hear your insights someday.

(*She slides it back to him. There is the sound of knocking.*)

OSCAR. My parents must be here.

(MS. MARTIN *gets up to leave,* THE FATES *follow her. She hesitates before exiting.*)

FATE #3. That's it, huh? Truly moving performance, especially considering you ruined his life.

MS. MARTIN. Don't let this define you Oscar.

(MS. MARTIN *exits, dialing a number on her phone as she does.*)

Scene 3

(*Lights up.* MS. MARTIN *is working at her desk.* THE FATES *are sitting off to the side, a bit more distant from* MS. MARTIN *than before, but still present.*)

MS. MARTIN. Come in.

MARIA. Hi, Ms. Martin.

MS. MARTIN. Hi, Maria. What can I—

MARIA. What happened to Oscar?

MS. MARTIN. Maria, I can't—

MARIA. I know! And I can guess what happened, but I just feel really bad. Oscar is a really nice person Ms. Martin, he wouldn't . . . do what he did without a good reason. I kind of feel like I snitched on him.

FATE #3. Awww, just like we did.

MS. MARTIN. I know what you mean.

(*They look sadly at one another for a beat.*)

MS. MARTIN. Actually, I could use your help.

MARIA. With what?

MS. MARTIN. I want to start some kind of program, in honor of Oscar. To make the school safer and more friendly. I was hoping you might want to help me.

MARIA. That sounds amazing. What did you have in mind?

MS. MARTIN. Well, I—

FATE #3. Why does she still want to talk to us? We don't have any good ideas.

FATE #2. If we even had a good idea, I'm pretty sure this school is way too underfunded. Where would we get the money?

(MS. MARTIN *falters for a moment.*)

FATE #1. Message from: Unknown number. Confirming therapy appointment with Dr. David on Wednesday, August 26th.

(MS. MARTIN *takes a deep breath and turns back to* MARIA.)

MS. MARTIN. Actually, I'd like to hear your ideas. I have a feeling you know what needs to change around here better than I do.

MARIA. Then why don't we get started?

(*Lights out.*)

End of Play

TOGETHA
by Azya Lyons

Cast of Characters

CHAYENNE, Dark-skinned African-American girl with crochet twists in her hair; in her late teens.

AIYANNA, Light-skinned African-American girl with a slick back ponytail; in her late teens.

IMANI, Dark-skinned African-American girl with dreads; in her late teens.

AALIYAH, Dark-skinned African-American girl with an afro updo; in her late teens.

Setting

Front yard of a house in the hood. A party commences behind the house (offstage).

Note

An alternate clean-language version of *Togetha* is available upon request. Contact Playscripts for more details.

Acknowledgments

Togetha was awarded a winner of the 2020 #ENOUGH: Plays to End Gun Violence competition and received further development with #ENOUGH: Plays to End Gun Violence (Michael Cotey, Producer). It was produced as part of #ENOUGH's Nationwide Reading and had its digital premiere produced by Alliance Theatre for Broadway on Demand on December 14, 2020. It was directed by Hananya Allen, Léa Fournier, Sam Provenzano and Anna Zheng; it was designed by Caroline Brown, Nicole Cortes, Chloe Lomax, and Fiona Tagami; editing by Nicky Taylor. The play was sponsored by Craig Kingsley. The cast was as follows:

CHAYENNE . . . . Colleen Allard-Smith
AIYANNA . . . . Tavin Bennett-Brown
IMANI. . . . . Khala Flemister
AALIYAH. . . . . LaNiyah S. Kelly

Required Program Credit

The digital premiere of *Togetha* was co-produced by #ENOUGH: Plays to End Gun Violence (Michael Cotey, Producer) and Alliance Theatre for Broadway on Demand.

TOGETHA
by Azya Lyons

(At rise: CHAYENNE, IMANI, and AALIYAH are seated on fold-up lawn chairs in the front yard, facing the audience. A fence with an open gate is on the proscenium line. Each girl has an empty plate and a water bottle at their feet. There is an empty chair beside IMANI for AIYANNA. Behind them is the house. It has faded yellow paint on the wall and burglar bars on the windows.)

(Lights up: The sound of laughter and loud music is in the background. A bouncy R&B song plays. THE GIRLS chatter inaudibly amongst themselves as AIYANNA enters stage right with a burger on a paper plate.)

CHAYENNE. Don't nobody care! Wear whatever you wanna wear, just don't be a hoe.

AIYANNA. *(Sitting down:)* Chay, be nice. *(Gesturing to IMANI:)* What's goin' on?

IMANI. *(Laughing:)* So, basically Aaliyah was like, "I wonder what I should take to school. I gotta find a man, ya'know?"

(AIYANNA takes a bite of the burger in her lap.)

IMANI. And Chay said that it don't matter, she ugly anyway. Then Aaliyah was like, "be serious, I don't wanna look like a hoe." Then Chay told her to not be a hoe.

AALIYAH. I really don't know why Chay is so mean to me. Like, I try to be nice and sweet or whateva, and all she do is bully me.

AIYANNA. *(Smiling:)* She loves you, Liyah, she's just naturally / mean—

CHAYENNE. Whatchu mean *(mocking AALIYAH:)* "I bully you?" *(She and AALIYAH begin laughing.)* Girl, dis ain't bullyin'. If you want me to, I will.

AALIYAH. *(To CHAYENNE:)* I'm just confused why you're clowning me.

CHAYENNE. *(To AIYANNA and IMANI:)* Y'all hear sum?

(AALIYAH rolls her eyes.)

AALIYAH. *(Suddenly serious:)* Bro, for real. Get off my ass.

CHAYENNE. *(Defensive:)* Ain't nobody on your ass, Aaliyah. Stop being a pussy.

IMANI. *(Holding her hands up:)* Chillllll, there's no need for allat.

AIYANNA. She just fuckin' witcha, Liyah. You know dat.

AALIYAH. *(Side-eyeing CHAYENNE:)* Yeah, I know. I jus' don' know why she bullyin' me so much today. Like, damn gir', lemme breathe.

CHAYENNE. I gotta give you sum to remember 'fore we leave.

(Everyone pauses, their faces falling, turning thoughtful. THE GIRLS let her words hang in the air.)

AIYANNA. *(Picking up her water bottle and taking a sip:)* It's weird, ain't it? We graduated today and I still feel da same. *(Taking a bite of her burger.)*

CHAYENNE. Aren't we 'posed to feel, like, grown?

IMANI. *(Mumbling:)* Ion feel grown at all.

AALIYAH. *(Looking at the water bottle at her feet:)* It's been eight years already?

CHAYENNE. *(Sighing:)* Yeah, we've been friends for 'bout eight years, now.

(No one speaks for a short period of time, reminiscing on their friendship.)

IMANI. *(Laughing, looking up to AIYANNA:)* Aye, Yanna. You remember when Chris lil ugly ass had a crush on you?

(CHAYENNE and AALIYAH suddenly howl in laughter as AIYANNA chokes.)

AIYANNA. *(Coughing:)* Don' remind me. *(Looks at THE GIRLS who are still laughing.)* Y'all, stop laughin'. It ain't funny. He was obsessed wimme!

CHAYENNE. *(Nasally with a lisp:)* Please Aiyanna! Just gimme a chance! I love you!

(AIYANNA hides her face in embarrassment.)

IMANI. *(In the same nasally lisp:)* Aiyanna! I brought you some chipth, but I ate them. I'm thorry.

(AALIYAH laughs loudly, her face reddening.)

AIYANNA. *(Slightly yelling:)* Y'all! Stopppp!

CHAYENNE. *(Cooing at AIYANNA:)* Awww, Aiyanna's embarrassed.

AIYANNA. *(Looking sourly at CHAYENNE:)* Okay, Miss "I'm Gonna Marry Coach Johnson".

IMANI. *(To AALIYAH:)* An' I, oop— *(They both laugh.)*

CHAYENNE. *(Smiling:)* Unh unh, don't do me, miss girl.

(AIYANNA *laughs.)*

CHAYENNE. *(Smiling:)* Hardy fucking har.

(The laughter dies down.)

Imma go get me some more water, *(to* AIYANNA*:)* gimme ya plate.

AIYANNA. *(Finishing her burger and giving* CHAYENNE *her plate:)* Thanks, b.

CHAYENNE. You good. *(Exits stage right.)*

(BEAT.)

IMANI. It's crazy to think that it's been eight years already. It feel like jus' yesterday we was in Ms. Walkah class.

AALIYAH. *(Shaking her head and smiling:)* That broad was crazy as a bitch, I swear to God.

(A relaxed rap song begins to play in the background.)

AIYANNA. *(Laughing:)* She was old as a bitch too.

(CHAYENNE *enters stage right and sits down.)*

AIYANNA. *(To* CHAYENNE*:)* We talkin' 'bout Ms. Walkah ol' ass.

CHAYENNE. *(Laughing:)* Brooo, fourf grade was wiillllld.

IMANI. Deadass, but it was good, ya'know?

(THE GIRLS nod in agreement.)

(BEAT.)

CHAYENNE. Did y'all hear about what happened wit Marcus and his girl?

AALIYAH. Nah! What happened?

IMANI. Didn't he, like, beat her or some shit?

CHAYENNE. Yeah, her brother came home to him hitting on her.

AIYANNA. Damn bro. That's fucked up.

CHAYENNE. *(Gesturing behind her:)* I just saw Unc' talking to him about "how to treat a woman." *(Laughing:)* He looked so miserable. *(Shaking her head:)* Forreal, Marie's way too good for him.

(THE GIRLS nod.)

(BEAT.)

IMANI. Y'all, ian tryna front, but I'm hella scared.

AIYANNA. *(Confused:)* Whatchu scared of?

IMANI. Of college and growin' up and shit. Like, jus' yesterday, we were fourf graders, meeting for the first time. An' now? Here we are, at our graduation party. Like, we di'n have enough time to figure all this shit out.

AALIYAH. *(Understandingly:)* I get that, sis. But, that typa min'set is gonna get you caught up. Don' think of it as tha end of high school. Think of it as the beginnin' of sum new. Of adulthood.

IMANI. *(Quietly:)* But ion know what comes wit' that. Tha's what I'm sayin'. I haven' had time to figure out what adulthood is yet.

(AIYANNA stands and goes behind IMANI, hugging her neck.)

CHAYENNE. Gir', we got plenty o' time. We'll figure it out togetha. I promise.

(AALIYAH and AIYANNA nod in agreement.)

IMANI. *(Patting AIYANNA's arm, reassured:)* Thank, y'all. Ian mean to, like, make this a sad moment.

AIYANNA. *(Straightening up and going to sit again:)* Girl, you good. Honestly, you should be excited about going to college.

IMANI. *(Confused:)* Whatchu mean?

AIYANNA. *(Smiling playfully:)* You can finally get away from that ugly ass boyfriend you got.

(CHAYENNE and AALIYAH crack up.)

IMANI. *(Mockingly:)* Ha ha. *(Smiling:)* You know he ain my boyfriend. We jus' talkin'.

AIYANNA. *(To CHAYENNE:)* You see how she ain' say he wasn't ugly?

IMANI. *(Laughing now:)* Leave him alone! He ain' ugly.

AALIYAH. He ain cute eitha.

IMANI. Oh whatever. Y'all jus' hard to please.

CHAYENNE. You just like ugly niggas.

(AIYANNA starts to hum along to the song. The sound of laughter and a grill are still loud behind them.)

(BEAT.)

IMANI. I'm lowkey excited, under all tha fear.

AALIYAH. Honestly, same. Like, I'm excited to not be in this dingy ass neighborhood no mo'. *(Looks around.)*

CHAYENNE. *(Nodding in agreement:)* Deadass. Like, I'll always have love for dis place, but it don' give us no options.

AIYANNA. You right. But, I mean, I wouldn' say that it don' have *no* options. We jus' don' have *enough* opportunities.

(THE GIRLS nod in agreement.)

(BEAT.)

(AIYANNA stands abruptly.)

AIYANNA. We got plenty o' time to think 'bout the future an' shit. Let's jus' enjoy this. Aight?

AALIYAH. *(Standing:)* You right. *(Exits stage right.)*

CHAYENNE. *(Watching AALIYAH walk away:)* Where she goin'?

(IMANI and AIYANNA shrug.)

Aight.

(A fast-paced contemporary R&B song plays in the background, louder than the other songs. AALIYAH enters stage right, an ear-to-ear grin on her face.)

AIYANNA. *(Standing and facing THE GIRLS:)* Yoooo, y'all remember when Maysie made us learn tha dance wit' ha?

AIYANNA. *(Laughing:)* Yeah, she thought Jamaal was gon' marry ha. We used to fight for him all tha time.

AALIYAH. *(Pointing at AIYANNA:)* Y'all was sleepin' on my man Marcus.

IMANI. So y'all jus' gon' forget that Jac was tha finest one in tha group?

CHAYENNE. *(Dancing:)* Y'all hoes blind, forreal.

IMANI. *(Turning to her:)* Ma'am, you can keep Ms. Ray Ray, okay?

(AIYANNA and AALIYAH burst out laughing.)

CHAYENNE. *(Stops dancing:)* He don' look like a girl! *(Beginning to dance again:)* He fine, you're jus' blind.

IMANI. *(Chuckling:)* I'm jus' sayin', we're here for ya wheneva you wanna come out.

CHAYENNE. *(Throwing her head back, laughing:)* Thanks.

AALIYAH. *(Looking into the distance:)* Who is dat?

CHAYENNE. *(Shrugging:)* Ion know. Don' one of y'all recognize tha car?

AALIYAH. *(Shaking her head:)* Nope.

(IMANI and AIYANNA shake their heads.)

CHAYENNE. It's good, they prolly jus' driving by.

(She goes back to dancing. IMANI and AIYANNA soon join her. AALIYAH keeps her eye on the approaching car.)

AIYANNA. *(Noticing AALIYAH:)* Liyah, relax. It's jus' a car.

AALIYAH. I'm tryna see if I can see who in there, Chay.

IMANI. Well, can ya?

AALIYAH. *(Focusing:)* Nah, not yet.

(Everyone continues to dance around her, CHAYENNE standing behind AIYANNA and IMANI. AALIYAH suddenly gets serious.)

AALIYAH. *(Squinting. confused:)* Ain't that Marie's bro—

(Then, fear and panic become evident on her face.)

AALIYAH. *(Holding her hand out, yelling:)* Wait—

(Four gunshots and the sound of tires screeching can be heard. CHAYENNE immediately falls to the ground, dead. THE GIRLS fall to the ground covering their heads.)

AIYANNA. *(Standing and walking to IMANI and holding out her hand:)* Holy shit, you good?

IMANI. *(Taking her hand:)* Yeah, I'm good.

(Behind them, AALIYAH crawls to CHAYENNE, who is still lying on the ground.)

AIYANNA. *(Angry:)* Who tha hell was that?

IMANI. *(Shrugging:)* Ion know.

(AALIYAH lets out a blood-curdling sob. AIYANNA and IMANI turn around, see CHAYENNE, and rush to her side.)

IMANI. Woah, what the fuck? Chay, you good?

AALIYAH. *(Sobbing:)* That bitch shot her, 'Mani. He— *(She sobs uncontrollably.)*

AIYANNA. *(Shocked:)* What? *(Shaking her head:)* No, stop playin'. *(Shakes CHAYENNE.)* Chay, get up. This ain funny, get cha ass up, Chay! *(Crying:)* Chay, stop playin. *(Shaking her harder.)*

IMANI. *(Under her breath:)* Holy shit. Holy shit. Holy shit. Holy shi—

(AALIYAH *sobs loudly, accompanied by* AIYANNA's *cries. The music in the background is still playing, but there is no more laughter.*)

IMANI. *(Voice breaking:)* Liyah?

(AALIYAH *looks at her.*)

IMANI. *(Quietly:)* Where was she shot?

(AALIYAH *points to the back of her head.* AIYANNA *cries harder.* IMANI *places her hand on the back of* CHAYENNE's *head gently. Her hand is red when she pulls it away.*)

IMANI. Holy shit. *(Staring in disbelief:)* Holy—

AIYANNA. *(Through tears:)* Oh my God!

AALIYAH. *(Voice breaking:)* We need to get somebody.

AIYANNA. *(Quietly:)* okay.

(*Suddenly,* IMANI *whips her phone from her back pocket.*)

IMANI. *(Voice breaking:)* I'm finna call somebody for help.

(AIYANNA *runs her hand over* CHAYENNE's *braids, whispering.*)

AIYANNA. *(Crying softly, to* CHAYENNE:) It's okay. She's gon' get you help. You'll be aight. I promise. You'll be aight again. *(Kissing* CHAYENNE's *hair:)* You're okay, Chay. You're gonna get to a hospital an' you're gonna be okay. Aight?

IMANI. *(Voice breaking:)* 'Yanna?

(AIYANNA *looks up at her.*)

I'm sorry. I shoulda— I didn't see—

(*Confused,* AIYANNA *shakes her head.*)

IMANI. *(Crying:)* I'm so so sorry. *(To* CHAYENNE:) I'm so so so sorry. *(She sobs loudly.*)

AIYANNA. *(Taking* AALIYAH's *hand in hers, voice shakey:)* It's okay, Liyah. You didn't know.

(AALIYAH *nods, still crying.* AIYANNA *cries, kissing* CHAYENNE's *hair and running her hand over it.*)

IMANI. *(Sniffling:)* Um, hello? I'm at 4535 Bradbury Drive and my friend just got shot . . . no ma'am. We're having a graduation party and someone just rode up and shot here . . . yes ma'am . . . 15 minutes? Why does it take so long?

(IMANI *looks over at the other girls, concern on her face.* AIYANNA *is speaking indistinctly as* AALIYAH *continues to sob silently.*)

IMANI. Okay. *(Beginning to cry:)* Please hurry. *(Pulling the phone away from her ear.)*

AIYANNA. *(Still running her hand over* CHAYENNE's *hair:)* It's okay, Chay. You're aight. I promise. You're good. You're safe.

(THE GIRLS *sit there, huddled around* CHAYENNE's *body.*)

(Lights out.)

End of Play

HULLABALOO
by Sarah Schecter

Cast of Characters

The Ringleader:

HUNTER, a charismatic man with a strong voice and shifty eyes. Wears a long coat and top hat, and holds a cane.

The Boys:

HOMER and MEL, a pair of teen boys/men. Homer is older than Mel.

Setting

The interior of a late 19th century big-top circus tent. Conveying this can be as simple as red and white drapes. In the center of the stage hangs The Curtain. Next to it, a throne like the Lincoln Memorial.

The Curtain:

A piece of cloth used to cover the grand finale and a portal used to project images and shadows/outlines behind it. Used for the Blood Map, which shows gun violence in the continental United States and beyond.

A Note from the Playwright

The show, Hunter's Hullabaloo, is a re-imagining of Buffalo Bill's storytelling and P. T. Barnum's grandeur, creating a fusion of American myth and gun culture.

The history included is adapted from information in the following sources:

Loaded: A Disarming History of the Second Amendment, by Roxanne Dunbar-Ortiz.

Out of Many, 5th edition, AP U.S. History textbook.

Know Your Enemy podcast. Episode "Gunpower" with Patrick Blanchfield.

Wikipedia pages on "Ringling Bros Circus," "Gun culture in the United States," "List of infantry weapons in the American Revolution."

Acknowledgments

Hullabaloo was awarded a winner of the 2020 #ENOUGH: Plays to End Gun Violence competition and received further development with #ENOUGH: Plays to End Gun Violence (Michael Cotey, Producer). It was produced as part of #ENOUGH's Nationwide Reading and had its digital premiere produced by Berkeley Repertory Theatre for Broadway on Demand on December 14, 2020. It was directed by Anthony A. Jackson; assistant directed by Si Mon' Emmett; video projections by Haley Miller; video editing by Benjamin Michel; sound design/editing by Courtney Jean. The play was sponsored by Rich Gillard. The cast was as follows:

HUNTER . . . . Jordan Winer
HOMER. . . . . Gabriel Vergez
MEL. . . . . Kevin Gill

Required Program Credit

The digital premiere of *Hullabaloo* was co-produced by #ENOUGH: Plays to End Gun Violence (Michael Cotey, Producer) and Berkeley Repertory Theatre for Broadway on Demand.

HULLABALOO
by Sarah Schecter

(While the audience gets seated, something like "Joshua Fit the Battle of Jericho" by Mahalia Jackson and something like "Big Iron" by Marty Robbins play on repeat.)

Hunter's Intro

(Lights dim. Something like "Reg'lar, Reg'lar, Rolling Under— Remastered" by Bessie Jones begins to play. A collage of firearm outlines is projected to fill The Curtain, almost glowing.)

(Lights come on and HUNTER enters, possibly through a tent flap. He taps The Curtain with his cane and the gun projection goes away. Drums, fanfare, or circus music sounds.)

HUNTER. Damn it. That's supposed to happen the other way around. Well hello, hello! Welcome out to *[Location]*, this *[Morning/ Afternoon/Evening]* gents and ladies. I am Hunter, also known as The Hunter—also known as Hunter Hank, and I am your ringmaster, your leader, your uncle, your guide and gent for this here traveling show. I sure am glad you put down your dime to see Hunter's Great Hullabaloo, the greatest show not just in the world—but in all of history. I am the wordsmith and ringleader for the brilliant acts you'll be seeing tonight. I'll show you the stories of this land you're sitting on, and the beasts that earned it, and what exactly made it so great.

While our acts are getting ready, you enjoy your peanuts and popcorn. I have a riddle for y'all. You gotta guess who I'm talking about. Whoever can put a name to the individual I'm describing will get a surprise.

(Turns around, and gets lost in his riddle, growing increasingly deranged. No longer cares about the comfort of his audience.)

HUNTER. I'm American like white crosses, red blood, and blue lives. I put the buckshot in your beef, the ball in your brain. Who was it that hushed the griot, shot Lincoln, the King and the Kennedys too? It was me, spreading like a fire on your prairie. Manifest destiny!

Fathered by Saxons and mothered by the Anglos, raised by the colonies, devourer of pheasant, pig and partridge, boars and bobcats, hippos and lions too, oh my! Conquered King Phil but rebuked by Pontiac. *(He mimes rock paper scissors with his hands.)* I beat steel, germs beat me.

61

HUNTER. Faithfully at the side of Daniel Boone and Jesse James, America fell in love with my voice years ago. Built to kill but fun for toys: six-shooters, powder caps, I dance on screens. Johnny Appleseed might have well planted bullets because I am everywhere.

Maybe I won't be in the news for a while, but I'll be around. I stand my ground.

Held by panthers or knights, you can try and coerce me with fire, water, and brute force—but my favorite amendment lets me do whatever I want.

I am well-oiled, ready to go, heavy with powder, the big iron on your hip, semi automatic and rapid-fire, double-barrelled, always loaded.

What's my name? Gatling, Smith, Wesson, Remington, Koch, Heckler, Colt, Beretta?

Call me the devil, but I'm just metal and wood! Who am I talking about?

(*He slumps, facing his feet. He reaches behind his back, very slowly.*)

HUNTER. ME! I'm talking about me! Hunter Hank, Uncle Sam, Brother Jonathan. I'm everybody! Anyone get it? Nobody got it, but that's OK. Sit tight! For the grandest show in history. All for you.

(*He ends with an Uncle Sam-esque point to the audience.* THE BOYS *enter, dressed in colonial settler clothing.*)

HOMER. ACT 1.

MEL. JUGGLING AND DANCES/COLONIAL TIMES.

HUNTER. I now present . . . The Juggling Jamestown Boys!

(HUNTER *hits* The Curtain *with his cane, and something like "Federal Overture" by Hesperus Early Music Ensemble begins to play.* HOMER *and* MEL *begin to do a dance in a classical colonial style to the music.* HUNTER *speaks along with the music.*)

HUNTER. Muskets, pistols, long rifles, knives, bayonets, tomahawks, axes, swords, sabres, pole arms and cannons, shot molds, tinder lighters and cartridge boxes too! Taking it back to the beginning, we had tools to get what we wanted all the way back when we first got here! Among other things guns really helped us expand, especially at first.

(*As he speaks, the* Blood Map *appears on* The Curtain. *Red splotches, like blood, spread across the map, Jamestown to the thirteen colonies, showing the growth of the United States from 1607 to 1853.)*

HUNTER. How many years was that, Mel?

MEL. Uh. Two hundred and sixty-four years!

HUNTER. Good boy. When was the first gun, Homer?

HOMER. The arquebus—a long-barreled, musket-like weapon—was most likely the first personal firearm on mainland America. Columbus and other early explorers were probably the first Europeans to bring firearms to the New World.

(HUNTER nods in approval. He snaps his fingers. THE BOYS pull out balls and begin to juggle.)

HUNTER. In the late 18th century, the Anglo-American settlers 'break-up from Britain came alongside the slaughtering of entire families without distinction of age or gender. This was the annihilation of what tribes, boys?

(THE BOYS start to toss the juggling balls back and forth, if they are in the same space. Their juggling display grows more and more impressive, getting taller and taller.)

THE BOYS. *(Alternating as they toss balls to each other:)* Cherokee, Muskogee, Delaware, Seneca, Mohawk, Miami, and Shawnee.

HUNTER. That's right. White Settler Militias expanded the boundaries of the thirteen colonies. Now, boys. In 1658, your home state of Virginia ordered every single settler to own a firearm! The government even provided loans for those who couldn't afford a weapon. What did this mean?

MEL. Taking land is an individual and collective right!

HOMER. A well-regulated militia!

HUNTER. Good! What else?

HOMER. Um. Sacred right to arm bears.

HUNTER. No, Homer!

MEL. No woman unarmed!

HUNTER. No, Mel! No *man* unarmed! Militias and armed households for the control of the land! Remember. What did I teach you two?

THE BOYS. EVERY MAN IS A SOLDIER.

HUNTER. Say it again!

THE BOYS. EVERY MAN IS A SOLDIER.

HUNTER. AGAIN!

(THE BOYS *fling their juggling balls up in the air and salute, letting the balls fall.*)

HUNTER + THE BOYS. EVERY MAN IS A SOLDIER.

(HUNTER *waves* THE BOYS *offstage. Still saluting, they begin to march offstage.*)

HOMER. ACT 2.

MEL. BEASTS/GUNSLINGERS.

(THE BOYS *exit.* HUNTER *hits The Curtain to stop the music.*)

HUNTER. Well. We've touched on covering the land, but how 'bout controlling it? Hunting is a classic pastime—one of my favorites—and a good way to keep things under control.

(HOMER *hands* HUNTER *a whip, taking away his cane.*)

(CRACK! *On The Curtain, the outlines of circus animals connected by chains run past. Sounds of a lion roaring, chains jingling, an elephant blowing its trumpet.*)

(CRACK! *A stampede of buffalo pass. Sounds of buffalo stampeding.*)

(CRACK! *A stampede of children pass. The sounds of children running and screaming.* HUNTER *shakes his head, and hits The Curtain until the kids disappear.*)

HUNTER. Oops. Things get a little crazy back there. Anyways, I've realized animals are smelly and ornery and really aren't that entertaining. We already killed all the buffalo, and no matter what anyone says, giraffe jerky is not nice. But you know what is? Bloodshed!

(CRACK! HUNTER *tosses whip offstage. Something like "I Walk The Line—Stereo Version" by Johnny Cash begins to play.* THE BOYS *enter in cowboy clothing and holsters.* MEL *hands* HUNTER *his cane. The three of them shuffle to the music.*)

HOMER. Yippee ki-yay!

HUNTER. Annie Oakley made sharpshootin' overrated. But a good old western standoff ain't! I've got the best two gunslingers here with us today, Homer and Mel, ready to shoot each other. Just for your entertainment! This act celebrates being an American in America, the land of low APR financin' and underseasoned meat! What else, fellas?

MEL. Supercuts!

HOMER. Key lime pie and Twinkies!

MEL. CVS!

HOMER. Diet soda!

MEL. Footlocker!

HOMER. Bass Pro shops!

MEL. Walmart!

HOMER. Goodyear tires!

HUNTER. That's right, boys! Now let's get a-shootin'.

> (*Music fades.* HOMER *and* MEL *face each other, slowly reaching back to holsters — only to pull out bananas.*)

MEL. What the hell is this?

HUNTER. Well. I can't actually have bullets flying about! You've gotta do that in private. I've got plenty of other stuff, though.

> (HUNTER *gestures to baskets on the ground, one next to* HOMER *and the other next to* MEL, *from which they pull out sticks shaped like guns, then hairdryers, then cell phones, then toilet plungers and Bibles — they aim them at each other then toss them aside.*)

HOMER. What do I have to do to get a goddamned gun around here?

HUNTER. Aw, it's too dangerous, Homer. The audience will love you anyways!

MEL. Well, those were all things the police have shot people for holdin'.

HUNTER AND HOMER. Shut up, Mel!

> (MEL *puts his hands up, rolling his eyes.*)

HOMER. It ain't a real gun show without guns, Hunter.

HUNTER. It ain't a real gun show without you two entertaining the audience!

MEL. It ain't about entertainment! It's about power.

HOMER. Right! Just 'cause you took us in doesn't mean anything. You just wanna entertain. We just wanna live the dream you promised us.

MEL. We're gonna find guns, old man!

HOMER. We'll have fun with them!

(HUNTER *shrugs.* HOMER *spits and* MEL *shakes his head. They exit.*)

HUNTER. I lead this show because people should know about the glory of our nation. They should *see* history. They should see its greatness. They should see people for who they are.

(*He pulls out a red clown nose, lipstick, and white powder, and begins to apply clown makeup as he speaks. He transforms into Uncle Sam. Projections appear on The Blood Map, showing the places he discusses.*)

HUNTER. You know, I'm a free thinker myself. I think about guns, and what they do. I've thought that maybe gun violence didn't necessarily start with gunpowder. Guns are their own beast, but just like race is born from racism, maybe guns are born from something besides metal.

Maybe gun violence was set up to be a problem back when gunpowder reached Europe, and when a papal decree in 1455 permitted the Portuguese monarchy to seize West Africa and enslave its population. Maybe policing was set up to be a problem when slave codes from the 1660s in the British colony of Barbados extended the task of controlling enslaved Africans from overseers and slavers to all white settlers. This meant collective racial policing was added to traditional English policing. This meant a tradition of settler terrorism, supported by guns.

Maybe the combination of guns and policing and industry were set up to be a problem with the capitalist firearm industry, which was among one of the first successful modern corporations. Gun proliferation and violence are among its legacies. But. Nobody's perfect, you know?

(*Beat.*)

I'm not here to just tell you my thoughts. I want *you* to be entertained. I want *you* to learn about guns. And the show must always go on. I'm sure you're all getting the best bang for your buck. The show must always go on.

(MEL *and* HOMER *run on stage and hand* HUNTER *his whip.*)

HOMER. ACT 3:

MEL. FREAKSHOW/CIVIL WAR.

(THE BOYS *exit. The sounds of a country night play; crickets and cicadas.* HUNTER *strolls back and forth with the whip. CRACK! Something like "Mean Old Bedbug Blues" by Furry Lewis begins to play.*)

HUNTER. This part used to be my favorite act of the whole thing. Fresh from Antietam, Bull Run, Gettysburg, Shiloh, Vicksburg. The freak show.

(*CRACK! He turns to The Curtain. There are outlines of limping and disfigured men walking behind the cloth, missing limbs, holding limbs, heads crooked. HUNTER looks at the figures hungrily with wide eyes. They pass and the music and night sounds fade.*)

HUNTER. But then it became illegal to show those guys. So we have to let you see 'em from behind a curtain, but it's really not the same. They're crumbling and too old to see— but there are still bodies like theirs. And you want to see the blood, and the gore. Just a peek. That's the thing about bad things. You can't help but watch! Sometimes that's what it means to be an American in America.

(*The Blood Map turns on, pulsing with every American mass shooting since 1999.*)

HUNTER. And sometimes it's not the gore you need to see, but just the constant possibility. That's what *was* entertaining about Annie Oakley's sharpshooting. She could shoot dimes from a man's hand, cigarettes from his lips, or the flame on a moving candle. She could shoot the middle of an ace of spades over her shoulder, looking in a mirror! Anything could happen.

Especially in ACT 4: TRAPEZE / SHARPSHOOTING. Now, this one is the greatest. It's my new favorite. Some folks will say America is committed to a social order predicated on human disposability. But I call it the greatest show in the greatest history of the greatest country on Earth!

(*Something like "Basin Street Blues" by Louis Armstrong begins to play. THE BOYS enter dressed in silk, and begin to perform incredible feats. HUNTER and the audience should both be in awe. HUNTER faces the audience, opening his arms. When the drum break begins, THE BOYS mime shooting machine guns at HUNTER, who shakes his body like it's being riddled with bullets.*)

(*Then, THE BOYS run forward with a gag. They come behind HUNTER. MEL takes his whip, and HOMER gags him. They tie him down in the throne, and an apple is placed on his head. MEL cracks the whip until the song turns off, faltering a few times.*)

MEL. I hate jazz.

HOMER. Me too, Mel. Well, I guess this is the real final act. You've taught us it takes fame to be a man, it takes infamy, it takes lives.

And you want to entertain 'em, don't you Hunter? We're American like white crosses, red blood, and blue lives.

You put the buckshot in our beef, the ball in our brain. Who was it that hushed the griot, shot Lincoln, the King and Hunter too?

> (MEL *cracks the whip, and something like "Stuck in the Middle with You" by Stealers Wheel begins to play.* MEL *pulls a mirror out of the sack and sets it in front of* HUNTER. MEL *and* HOMER *pull white robes out of their clothes, and put them on.* HOMER *pulls out a gun-shaped package from his robe.* HOMER *hands it to* MEL, *and puts his hand on* MEL's *shoulder.*)

> (*A red laser target lights up on* HUNTER's *forehead. The Curtain finally lifts up, revealing a field of objects: a baby crib, a dummy at a high school desk, a white cross, a rainbow flag, a Torah, a teddy bear in a chair—all with their own laser targets aimed at them. The light gets brighter and brighter, focusing on the Curtain, now an enormous American flag hanging above everything at the center of the stage. The light gets brighter and brighter until the room is flooded with white light.*)

End of Play

GHOST GUN
by Olivia Ridley

Cast of Characters

BLACK BOY, 18. Played by a black actor.

Setting

Setting here is ambiguous. Play is performed facing the audience.

Notes on Language

Modifications for profanity:

Page	Original	Modification
2	"You're all scared shitless."	"Y'all are scared, now."
2	"Same damn thing."	"Same thing."
3	"Apparently that 'mentally ill' shit don't apply to brown skin."	"Apparently 'mentally ill' don't apply to brown skin."
4	"I seem to be the only one who sees this shit."	"I seem to be the only one who sees any of this."
5	"Steeped in it like a fuckin' teabag."	"Steeped in it like a teabag.
5	*(Sucks teeth)* "Fuck this."	*(Sucks teeth)* "Screw this."

Acknowledgments

Ghost Gun was awarded a winner of the 2020 #ENOUGH: Plays to End Gun Violence competition and received further development with #ENOUGH: Plays to End Gun Violence (Michael Cotey, Producer). It was produced as part of #ENOUGH's Nationwide Reading and had its digital premiere produced by Goodman Theatre for Broadway on Demand on December 14, 2020. It was directed by Ken-Matt Martin; video/projection design Yee Eun Nam; sound design Twi McCallum; editing Cody Nieset. The play was sponsored by Erin Ogletree. The cast was as follows:

BLACK BOY . . . . .Jayson Lee

Required Program Credit

The digital premiere of *Ghost Gun* was co-produced by #ENOUGH: Plays to End Gun Violence (Michael Cotey, Producer) and Goodman Theatre for Broadway on Demand.

GHOST GUN
by Olivia Ridley

(Lights up on BLACK BOY, clad in all black, sweatshirt and jeans. He wears dark sunglasses, his hood up, and a black bandana covers his mouth. He is noticeably upset/anxious, maybe pacing and trying to collect himself. There is a handle sticking out of his jeans pocket. He is inferred to be carrying a gun. After standing in front of the audience for maybe 10–15 seconds, he tears off the hood, the gloves, the sunglasses, like it's choking him. He is desperate to get it off. The bandana is the last thing he tears down.)

BLACK BOY. You see me? *You see me?* My flesh is *rotting.* My flesh—

I got a gun now. Of course y'all see me. You all couldn't help but see me now. You're all scared shitless.

So you sit, waiting for the villain's monologue before he shoots you, before he shoots the *heroes,* and you won't dare interrupt. But who's hero, and who's villain, *really?*

You want a reason. No—you want a story. Yeah, you want a real sob story, or just a *good* one, one worth your last few minutes on earth

You ask for the tragic backstory.

You hear me start, poverty, gangs, blah blah blah. What's new, black boy? We want something new. Something *fresh.* Something *exciting.*

(BLACK BOY looks down at the gun tucked in his pants.)

So what about black boy gets a gun? Black boy gets power? Black boy gets *seen?* Black boy can command a room, like I'm a rich, billionaire CEO or something, in a room with his insects for employees, telling 'em who's getting fired and who's not. You can find the same kinda power in a gun, man. Same damn thing. And it's a hell of a lot easier for black boy to get a gun than for him to become any kind of CEO.

(Beat.)

You ask me why. Why the gun, why now, and you'll know with time. But I can tell you what it's not, apparently:

Did y'all know that black boys can't get mental illness? 'Cause apparently that "mentally ill" shit don't apply to brown skin. Anxiety, depression, bipolar, addiction, they don't count when they occupy black bodies. *Especially* not addiction, nah, that's not an illness. It's the . . . constant replenishment of good, that just also happened to be a little bad, right?

BLACK BOY. 'Cause when you alive, when you *really* alive, the ugly is inescapable. It runs in rivers in blood soaked streets. Hangs low in smoggy, cancer-filled air. Floats in the harsh stench of urban decay. 'Cause that's what the hood's like sometimes. And that's all y'all "see" about it too:

Something dirty, something rotting. And y'all still dare to smile.

The thing is, you don't see it. 'Cause if you saw it, you *really* saw it, you couldn't smile.

Those addicts? They see it. They *alive*. Shocked back awake every single time that needle hit their vein. So that's where they got their good. They couldn't bear the bad.

They're weak like that.

But me? I wouldn't miss your slow, steady, silent destruction—I wouldn't miss it for the world.

I am stronger than that. Better, than that. So I sat silent, watching you bring yourselves and everyone around you to ruin.

    (Short beat.)

But no one saw me though. *Really saw me,* I mean. See, I got to be a new kind of invisible, cause y'all still saw me. Oh y'all *definitely* saw me. The more I hid my face, the more scared you were, so you saw me to keep *yourself* safe, and that's the only reason you wanted to see me. To be cautious.

My kind of invisible, it's a little different. Like you can't help but notice me in a room, but it's a I-could-get-shot-in-the-street-tomorrow-and-no-one-would-look-twice, kind of invisible. You'd see it, sure. The crack of the bullet, sharp bend of my knees, the dark, wet pavement, the stillness. The stillness. You'd see it, sure. But the shock's not there. The falling of black bodies—that's just a side effect of livin' in the ghetto, right? It's they fault for living there, getting all, wrapped up in it. There is no outrage. Just a vague, unpleasant taste in your mouth. You change the channel.

That's where the invisibility comes in: it would mean nothing to you. Too common. Lacks . . . *shock factor.* Just to be expected of such a violent, aggressive race, right? They the reason the ghetto's like that in the first place. Why it makes you feel *uncomfortable* and *unsafe.* It's not the poverty that gives rise to crime—no, it is *them.* Why pretend it amounts to anything more than what it is: something ugly, something born from their own, inherently ugly race. Decomposition is a natural process. Why try to stop it?

    (Short beat.)

BLACK BOY. I am disgusting. I know it, too, and y'all made sure I did. And that disgust, that . . . repulsion, it seeps into your veins and consumes your body like a tumor. And so I've started to rot. And no one wants to come near rotting flesh.

(Low, hurting, introspective:) That's my kind of invisible. I mean nothing to no one.

(Short beat.)

(Growing aggression:) You all could go to hell. It's me—I am the only one who sees anything. And NO ONE understands that. I'll stand here, and I'll monologue about the death, about the destruction, about how you all are doomed, how you are *sprinting* towards your demise, and y'all won't hear a thing. *I* am the only one. I am the ONLY ONE who listens. I'm the ONLY ONE who sees. I am the ONLY ONE who knows. *(Explodes:)* I AM ALL SEEING. I AM YOUR GOD.

> *(Stops suddenly, growing conscious of his hysteria. Calms down, brief chuckle.)*

You know, I could've shot you all already. Y'all see my gun. That's how I introduced myself before, remember? And I'm sure that's all y'all could look at. Still missin my flesh as always, my face, my body, distracted by something flashier, shinier, something with power: like a gun. But I don't mind. In fact, I *get* it.

But in all your *staring*, your *awe*, did y'all look close enough? Notice anything? A tiny little design, a little detail . . .

> (BLACK BOY *takes gun out and shows it to audience, revealing an orange marking on barrel. The gun is comically and very obviously fake, put together with black duct tape, etc.)*

BLACK BOY. Orange tape. *(Biting:)* It's *fake*.

And so my power, it dissipates into thin air like it never was. I'm back to being nothing. But at least I got y'all's attention, right? You listening?

'Cause I need you to hear me say: Killing you all would do no good. I don't need a gun, and y'all don't need bullets in your head. 'Cause get this: y'all *been* dead. I seem to be the only one who sees this shit. We are *crumbling*. We are *doomed*.

'Cause y'all . . . y'all spill blood in invisible ink. Not to hide it from anyone else but yourselves. God forbid you see a little red, worry your little heads about the ugly. And in not seeing it, you perpetuate the ugly, you *become* the ugly. Wake up, kill a little bit, all with empty eyes and an absent smile, wipe your bloodied hands at the end of the day, go to bed, repeat. And repeat. And repeat cause, 'cause you didn't *have* to see the ugly. You had the privilege of choice.

BLACK BOY. But the ugly: the ugly was my entire life, man. That's *all* I am. That's all I see. The *ugly*. I can't change channels like y'all can. I see black bodies fall whether I want to or not. And if—or whenever—I'm shot by someone, when my knees bend sharp, and my black body falls, and I'm suddenly still, I will bleed, and it will be red, and it will be sure, and it will be inescapable.

I will lie there crooked, body mangled, and the sight of me will be something unbearable. Bleeding black bodies are ugly. *I* am the ugly y'all seem to need to shield yourself from. Steeped in it like a fuckin' teabag.

And that's the only way you live. You all killed yourselves so you wouldn't have to look at it but me, I stare ugly right back in its eyes. God doesn't step down from ugly. God can't. God *is* ugly.

(Slowly, with intention:) So I'll cock my ghost gun 'cause that's all I need. Y'all are dead already, with or without a metal bullet in your head.

> (BLACK BOY *begins to study his gun.*)

(Sucks teeth:) Fuck this. *(Quick change in pace:)* Y'know, I got the real thing back home. Cause that glittering, black metal, the power, this . . . primal obsession with the power to kill so swiftly; it's *intoxicating,* man. So I say: give me something to shoot. Let me utilize this power. And I think, I think to myself, if everybody's dead already, if everybody's gone, well, well who's left to shoot then?

> (BLACK BOY *continues studying gun, turning it in his hands. Accidentally ends up with it pointed at self. Brief chuckle. Through the following, he allows the gun [not necessarily its tip] to graze/ wander around his chest, face, etc.)*

It's not fair, you know. That I can smell your rotting insides. *(Slowly, deliberately:)* Flies gather in your stomach, seduced by the green and white spores that have blossomed in your ribcage like flowers. But they've somehow missed the flesh, and it remains pristine.

> *(Puts gun down.)*

Untainted. Approachable. Y'all get to be happy, you know.

(With deep, immutable hurt:) How could it be fair, that even though all y'all are the dead ones, that mine is the only corpse rotting?

> *(LIGHTS OUT.)*

End of Play

GUNS IN DRAGONLAND
by Eislinn Gracen

Cast of Characters

LILAH GORDON, female. Third-grader. Imaginative, innocent, headstrong, tomboyish. Usually plays on the playground alone. A brilliant, young mind. The princess of the dragons.

TOUCAN, any. An imaginary dragon. A playful parental type. As colorful as their name suggests.

Setting

Present Day
Anytown, USA
Any elementary school's playground and hallway/Dragonland

Note

A "/" in a line signifies the next character interrupting. Anything after the "/" is what the current character means to say. A "/" before a character's line means that they are the one to interrupt the preceding character.

Acknowledgments

Guns in Dragonland was awarded a winner of the 2020 #ENOUGH: Plays to End Gun Violence competition and received further development with #ENOUGH: Plays to End Gun Violence (Michael Cotey, Producer). It was produced as part of #ENOUGH's Nationwide Reading and had its digital premiere produced by Orlando Repertory Theatre for Broadway on Demand on December 14, 2020. It was directed by Samantah Reser; lighting design by Kyle Wiehe. The play was sponsored by Tom and Colette Walls. The cast was as follows:

     LILAH............................ Hannah Kovacic
     TOUCAN .... Caroline Brett

Required Program Credit

The digital premiere of *Guns in Dragonland* was co-produced by #ENOUGH: Plays to End Gun Violence (Michael Cotey, Producer) and Orlando Repertory Theatre for Broadway on Demand.

GUNS IN DRAGONLAND
by Eislinn Gracen

(A school bell rings.)

(Sounds of children shouting and laughing is heard. It's recess time.)

(LILAH, a young girl, bolts onstage, grabs a stick from off the ground, and runs to a piece of playground equipment. She stands on top of it triumphantly.)

LILAH. *(Shouting:)* I am Lilah Gordon, the princess of Dragonland, and you shall listen to me, dragon!!

(A dragon, TOUCAN, appears dramatically, growling and snarling fiercely as they approach her. LILAH wears a smug look of bravery on her face.)

TOUCAN. RAAGH! ROOOOOARR!! BOOGA BOOGA!!

(TOUCAN pounces, enveloping LILAH in a giant bear hug from behind.)

LILAH. Oh, Toucan!

TOUCAN. Did I getcha this time?

LILAH. No, of course not. You never do. You don't scare me, beast! You haven't scared me since we started playing together on the first day of school!

(Beat.)

I feel like it's my job as princess of the dragons to not be *afraid* of any dragons.

(LILAH shows off her "sword.")

TOUCAN. Ah, grr. I suppose you're right. One of these days I'll catch you off-guard.

(Beat.)

Hey, what're we doing today, Lilah?

LILAH. We can climb the castle spire of the jungle gym!

TOUCAN. Nah, we did that Wednesday.

LILAH. We can . . . play fireball!

TOUCAN. No way, I threw my wing out last time we played. This five-hundred-and-nine-year-old physique isn't what it used to be.

LILAH. Oh, yeah! You got it caught in the soccer net. I remember going to the nurse for you but she wouldn't give me ice for you because it was "a waste."

TOUCAN. Grr. That's right. No-good non-believin' crone.

(Sounds of children playing together are heard. LILAH is distracted by them.)

TOUCAN. Say, what are they doing over there with that ball? Looks pretty dangerous and violent. Let's go play!

LILAH. No. I don't wanna play with them.

TOUCAN. Aw, man. It looks so fun! Why not?

LILAH. They've been mean. I don't really wanna talk about it.

TOUCAN. You know that you can tell me anything, right?

LILAH. Yeah, I know. That's why I'd much rather play with you.

(LILAH eyes the empty swing set.)

Ooh! Can we have flying lessons?

TOUCAN. Well, maybe for a little bit. I don't wanna waste our daily thirty minutes on something too dangerous.

LILAH. Yessss.

(LILAH runs over and stands on top of a swing. TOUCAN stands behind her and begins to push. LILAH awkwardly gains height, when she's at an average distance she jumps off, falling to the ground gracelessly.)

LILAH. Ow, ow, owww.

TOUCAN. Ah, gorgon brains, I knew this was a bad idea. We really should've learned after the last five times it ended this way. Where does it hurt?

LILAH. *(Tearfully:)* My leg, my knee.

TOUCAN. Gotcha. Just lemme do my thing.

(TOUCAN mystically "heals" LILAH's leg.)

LILAH. Thanks, Toucan. I just don't understand why flying never works for me.

TOUCAN. Oh, Lilah. We've been over this, humans can fly about as well as a phoenix can swim.

LILAH. Well, I wanna be the best flying human! How did you get your wings? Hmm? *Hmm?*

TOUCAN. Ugh, it's a pretty long tale.

LILAH. Don't feel bad, I love your tail! It's so nice and warm it feels like a pillow made out of jeans and old people skin.

TOUCAN. No, no, no. I mean *tale*. Like a story. It's a pretty long, boring story.

LILAH. Please? Pretty please with a fish on top?

TOUCAN. Well all right, the fish on top convinced me. If you must know, it was my three hundredth or so birthday and I was trapped-deep down inside this cave of goblins / and . . .

LILAH. / Three hundred!? That's like, three hundred more years away until I get my own wings!

TOUCAN. Hey, hey, hey, look at you, someone's been paying attention in math.

    (Beat.)

Personally, I don't believe that age has anything to do with it. You see, in that cave I helped those goblins by finding a magic amulet of peace or something, long story. But anyways, I got my wings that day because I performed a *valiant action*.

LILAH. That's how I'll learn to fly! I'll get my wings when I perform a gelatin action.

TOUCAN. Valiant, hun.

LILAH. C'mon, let's go perform an action before recess is over. I already see kids lining up.

TOUCAN. All right, you're the boss, princess.

    (LILAH looks at the ground in search for an adventure. She stumbles across an anthill.)

LILAH. Ah! Toucan, right here! There's a thousand and one army of insectoids who want to steal the kingdom's food! We have to stop them!

    (LILAH eagerly runs over to a nearby ant pile. She prepares to stomp on it.)

TOUCAN. Whoa, whoa, whoa. Hold your centaurs. These hungry insectoid soldiers aren't doing anything wrong. They're completely defenseless. How would you feel if someone a hundred times bigger stepped on you?

LILAH. *(Under breath:)* I wouldn't like it very / much.

TOUCAN. / You wouldn't like it very much, would you? Yeah. That's what I thought.

LILAH. Oh Toucan this is useless, there's nothing battalion to do here and everyone's already going back inside.

TOUCAN. Valiant. And these things take time, I'll see you tomorrow girlie-q. Pay attention in math.

LILAH. No wait, Toucan. I just got an idea. What if I hid here? We could have so much more time to think of heroic things to do.

TOUCAN. Oooh! What a fun idea! Let's do it!

(LILAH *hides underneath* TOUCAN's *wings. Beat. She pokes her head back out.*)

LILAH. Awesome! We did it! Now what?

TOUCAN. I was gonna ask you the same thing.

(A *distant, discombobulated, semi-mechanical roaring noise stops the duo.*)

LILAH. Woah! What was that?!

TOUCAN. No idea. I don't see any dark clouds, can't be an angry thunder dragon.

LILAH. Maybe it's a hurt unicorn!

TOUCAN. That didn't sound like any unicorn I've ever heard before.

LILAH. Are you okay, Toucan? I've never seen you so nervous before.

TOUCAN. What? Oh, yeah. I guess I'm just a little uneasy is all.

(LILAH *hugs* TOUCAN *from behind.*)

LILAH. I love you, Toucan. There's nothing to be afraid of.

TOUCAN. I love you too, Lilah. Your hugs make me feel like I can do anything.

LILAH. Good! Because I have a feeling that our next quest has to do with that noise!

TOUCAN. (*Disturbed:*) Oh. All right. I guess we're going into the school after all, huh?

LILAH. Yup! Let's go save that creature! Or defeat it! Whichever comes first!

TOUCAN. Whichever comes first!

(TOUCAN *notices* LILAH's *stick on the ground.*)

TOUCAN. Oh, hang on.

(TOUCAN *picks up the stick.)*

Your sword, princess?

LILAH. Ah, yes. My swordy-sword. The most valuable relic in all of Dragonland.

(LILAH *and* TOUCAN *admire the "blade.")*

Now that I have my weapon, let's be off!

TOUCAN. *(Like a pilot:)* How are we traveling today, co-pilot Lilah?

LILAH. *(Like a pilot:)* I think we should teleport today, co-pilot Toucan, over.

TOUCAN. Kshhh. Sounds like a plan. Kshhh. Prepare for takeoff, over.

(*The duo begin to spin in place as if they're "teleporting." They are interrupted by the same sound from earlier, only it's a bit more clear. Distant screams.* TOUCAN *lands on their butt.)*

TOUCAN. Crash landing, crash landing! Mayday, mayday! Anything but that awful sound again!

LILAH. Only it was different this time. I think I heard some people scream. Oh, Toucan. We've gotta save them! Maybe they lost their magic amulet of peace, like in your story!

TOUCAN. It could be many things. Many things a young princess is not prepared for. My worry is that this is the mark of a Death Dragon. They've become more and more common in recent years.

LILAH. Whoa, Death Dragon? Awesome!

TOUCAN. No, not awesome. Terrifying. Death Dragons hurt innocents purely because they can. I don't want to get you involved with a beast like that. We should go somewhere else.

LILAH. Toucan, if I'm ever gonna be the perfect princess of Dragonland, I need to perform my *valiant* action and earn my wings! This is the perfect opportunity. I feel like you don't even want me to.

TOUCAN. Of course I want to, Lilah. I just have a nasty feeling.

LILAH. I'm going in. They need me.

TOUCAN. Lilah, I'm very sorry that running is not the game you want to play right now, but sometimes we have to play games that we hate.

LILAH. What if it's not a Death Dragon? Why would a Death Dragon ever kill another dragon?

TOUCAN. Your guess is as good as mine.

LILAH. Well, if it is a Death Dragon like you say it is, we can use our power of friendship to make him good, y'know?

TOUCAN. You might be onto something there.

LILAH. If we can show it our friendship power, then we can save Dragonland and the school!

TOUCAN. You're right!! C'mon let's teleport in there, quickly!

(Silence. The lights inside the school are completely shut off. LILAH stumbles into a locker. It is dead silent as she continues to explore her space.)

LILAH. Hello? Where did everyone go?

(Beginning to panic:)

Toucan, I'm scared.

TOUCAN. Aw honey, there's nothing to, uh, be afraid of here.

LILAH. *(Overwhelmed with fear:)* Toucan? Toucan? Where are you?

TOUCAN. Lilah? I don't believe we're playing hide and seek are we? I'm right here!

LILAH. I want Mommy!! I want Daddy!! Where are they? This isn't normal!

TOUCAN. Lilah, Lilah! I'm right here! Listen to me! Lilah!!

(The light on LILAH dulls. She has been sucked back into reality. TOUCAN tries to console her only to find that they no longer can touch her. Footsteps. LILAH nervously rises to her feet. TOUCAN continues to attempt connection. More footsteps. LILAH reacts to the unseen Death Dragon; Be it a step forward or other movement. A low growl reverberates the room. Perhaps fog. The lights fade in all spots except for LILAH's face. He is the epitome of what should be feared. She looks up at him.)

LILAH. I am Lilah Gordon, princess of th−!

(The sound of a cocked gun is heard. The trigger is pulled, emitting a massive ear-shattering dragon roar. LILAH has been shot. Complete Blackness. Eventually a light starts to grow on LILAH, ending in a spectacular burst of flickering light. With the return of light emerges LILAH's new wings. LILAH, now reawakened, has

completed her valiant action. TOUCAN *and* LILAH *can now see each other again. They embrace.)*

LILAH. I am Lilah Gordon. And I was the Princess of the Dragons.

*(*LILAH *looks at the sky above her and prepares to fly upwards.)*

End of Play

Epilogue

Since we began . . .

8 Americans have been shot and wounded.

4 more Americans were killed with guns.

And sometime between then and the next 90 minutes,

1 person on the age of 19 will be killed with a gun.

For too many, the story of gun violence isn't fiction, it's a reality.

Each of these plays was around 10 minutes.

10 minutes isn't all that long.

And to address something as huge as gun violence, 10 minutes might not feel like enough time at all.

But on October 1st, 2017, ten minutes was long enough for a gunman to kill 60 people and wound 411 others in Las Vegas.

And on December 14th, 2012, half that amount of time—only 5 minutes—was long enough for a gunman to kill 20 children and 6 adults at Sandy Hook Elementary School.

We live in a country where so many lives can be stolen in 10 minutes or less,

But maybe 10 minutes of a *moving story* can also be enough—

Enough to change hearts

And enough to change minds.

Because if numbers and statistics *were* enough,

We wouldn't all have to be here to *say*—

"ENOUGH."

Playwright Biographies

Adelaide Fisher is a Florida-based writer. She wrote this play with the support of the Orlando Repertory Theater. She's been involved in theatre since she was five, and wrote her first play in the seventh grade for Young Playwrights for Change. Right now, you can find her both onstage and behind the scenes proudly representing International Thespian Troupe 6614. When she's not at rehearsal, she spends her time reading, baking, studying, and doing art. She lives with her mom, her dad, her younger brother, and two pet snails, named Velma and Daphne.

Eislinn Gracen is Florida-based artist and writer. Her piece, *Guns in Dragonland,* was initially workshopped and produced as a virtual staged reading as the headliner for Beth Marshall Presents' New Works Series. She was a participant and winner in the inaugural Be Original playwriting festival in 2019, hosted by New Generation Theatricals and Dr. Phillips Performing Arts Center. She won the Florida Theatrical Association Award for her play, *Wolf in a Concrete Jungle,* which was performed as a table read at the festival and also as a staged reading at UCF last winter. Most recently, she wrote the part of The Pardoner in the Howler's Theatre presented virtual reading of the Orlando Fringe Festival's *The Canterbury Tales Project.*

Azya Lyons is a Mississippi-based creative writer. She enjoys writing fiction, creative nonfiction, and poetry and plans to make writing her vocation. Azya is the recipient of two Silver Keys in Scholastics, has been published in two literary journals, and has won a national poetry contest.

Debkanya Mitra is a Maryland-based writer and is currently a student at the University of Maryland.

Olivia Ridley is a New Jersey-based writer. In 2018, her play *Slush,* which explored the similarly topical issue of assisted suicide, was selected to be performed at Luna Stage in NJ. Though she is deeply passionate about playwriting, she also has a more extensive background as a performer, working primarily with Vanguard Theater Company in NJ. And her passions extend beyond theater; she loves writing/performing slam poetry when she can, and enjoys political science and debate as well. In her art, Olivia hopes to expose the nuance of "taboo" topics and spark much needed conversation, seeking to educate not only the audience, but herself as well in the process.

Sarah Schecter is a theatre artist, community organizer, and chef from Oakland, California. She is a member of the Teen Core Council at Berkeley Repertory Theatre. Her work has been published by the *New York Times*, Still I Rise Films, and We Write The World, and performed by Oakland School for the Arts, PlayGround SF, and the Heart of Oakland Festival. She spends her non-theatrical time as President of Bay Area Student Activists, a student-led civic engagement group, and learning and cooking in kitchens around the Bay Area.

Elizabeth Shannon is a Maryland-based writer. She is an apprentice at the Maryland Ensemble Theatre (MET), as well as a member of the Theatre Focus in the Academy for the Fine Arts. Her play, *What Are You Hiding?*, which she co-wrote with Morgan Southwell, was a winner of Baltimore Centerstage's Young Playwright's Festival, and a finalist in The Secret Theatre's Act One: One Act Festival, as well as part of the live-streamed reading series, *The Future Was Now*, by Quarantined Theatre Company, which can be found on YouTube. Her play, *Smoke*, has also been published through Scripts For Stage, and had a Zoom performance with University of Texas El Paso's student organization, Ensemble. Her play, *Nuclear* is a current winner of The Blank Theatre's 28th Annual Young Playwrights Festival.

#ENOUGH Nationwide Reading

The plays in this anthology received simultaneously staged readings in 50 communities in 25 states and on three continents on December 14, 2020—the 8-year remembrance of the shooting at Sandy Hook. Over 1,100 artists were involved from the following theatres, schools, and community organizations:

1st Stage (Tysons, VA)

AIM Academy, + Students Demand Action Philly (Conshohocken, PA)

Alumni Theater Company (Pittsburgh, PA)

American Blues Theater (Chicago, IL)

American Stage Education (St. Petersburg, FL)

Azuka Theatre + InterAct Theatre Company + Dramatists Guild (Philadelphia, PA)

Bag&Baggage Productions (Hillsboro, OR)

Barnegat High School (Barnegat, NJ)

Baumholder MHS (Germany)

Canyon View High School (Cedar City, UT)

Cape Cod Community College (West Barnstable, MA)

Capital High School (Olympia, WA)

Carthage College (Kenosha, WI)

Celebration Company at the Station Theatre (Champaign, IL)

Center Stage Theater + UCSB Initiative for New & Reimagined Work (Santa Barbara, CA)

Centre Stage (Greenville, SC)

Colorado Springs Fine Arts Center + Colorado Theatre Guild + Dramatists Guild of Colorado (Colorado)

Edison Eagle Theatre (Tulsa, OK)

Globe Online (Fairfax, VA)

Hall High School (West Hartford, CT)

Hanover High School Footlighters (Hanover, NH)

Honolulu Theatre for Youth + graduates from the National School of Drama (Honolulu, HI + Agartala, Tripura, India)

Kitchen Dog Theater (Dallas, TX)

Lake Zurich High School (Lake Zurich, IL)

Long Beach Polytechnic High (Long Beach, CA)

Madison Uphoff (Madison, WI)

Masters School (Dobbs Ferry, NY)

Mildred's Umbrella Theater Co. (Houston, TX)

Mile Square Theatre (Hoboken, NJ)

Mosaic Theater of DC (Washington, DC)

Patriot Productions (Freehold, NJ)

Portland Public Schools + Artists Repertory Theatre + The Acting
Conservatory (Portland, OR)

Rose Theater (Omaha, NE)

San Bernardino High School Theatre (San Bernardino, CA)

Santa Fe Playhouse (Santa Fe, NM)

Shakespeare Studio (Montgomery, WV)

South Bend Civic Theatre (South Bend, IN)

South Milwaukee High School (South Milwaukee, WI)

Teatro Quetzal (El Paso, TX)

Teatro Visión (San José, CA)

Third Avenue Playhouse (Sturgeon Bay, WI)

Third Rail Repertory Theatre (Portland, OR)

Trinity Rep (Providence, RI)

UNI Multicultural Theatrical Society (Cedar Falls, IA)

Waukee Thespian Troupe #1452 (Waukee, IA)

West Orange High School (West Orange, NJ)

Westmont High School (Campbell, CA)

Wilbury Theatre Group (Providence, RI)

Wisconsin Council of Churches (Madison, WI)

Youth Performing Arts School (Louisville, KY)

About #ENOUGH: Plays to End Gun Violence

Founded in 2019 by Michael Cotey, #ENOUGH: Plays to End Gun Violence calls on teens to confront gun violence by creating new works of theatre that will spark critical conversations and inspire meaningful action in communities across the country. #ENOUGH's mission is to promote playwriting as a tool for self-expression and social change, harnessing this generation's spirit of activism and providing a platform for America's playwrights of tomorrow to discover and develop their voices today. Learn more: www.enoughplays.com.

Michael Cotey (Founder & Producer)

Si Mon' Emmett (Program Associate)

#ENOUGH Advisory Council

Alvaro Saar Rios (Playwright)
Barbara Pitts McAdams (Co-Creator, #HereToo Project)
Bill Rauch (Artistic Director, Perelman Center for the Arts)
Hallie Gordon (Director & Producer)
Idris Goodwin (Playwright & Director, Colorado Springs Fine Arts Center)
John Weidman (Librettist & Book Writer)
Jonathan Shmidt Chapman (Executive Director, Theatre for Young Audiences/USA)
Mara Richards Bim (Artistic Director, Cry Havoc Theater)
Michael Rohd (Artistic Director, Sojourn Theatre Company)
Sarah Ruhl (Playwright)
Willa Taylor (Walter Director of Educations & Engagement, Goodman Theatre)

#ENOUGH 2020 Selection Committee

David Henry Hwang
Karen Zacarías
Lauren Gunderson
Robert Schenkkan
Tarell Alvin McCraney

2020 Campaign Sponsors

Broadway on Demand
Playscripts
The Dramatists Guild

Special thank you to the many theatre professionals below who volunteered their time to be readers for #ENOUGH:

Adam Marier

Allie Bonesho

Amanda Gladu

Andrew Acevedo

Andrew Clancey

Arya Daire

Bex Ehrman

Bryce Lord

Caitlin Lowans

Casey Hoekstra

Cathlyn Melvin

Cody Proctor

David Kersnar

Deborah Clifton

Edward Morgan

Eva Nimmer

Gaby Sant'Anna

Grace DeWolff

Gregg Benkovich

Guy Massey

Izaiah Ramirez-Ealy

Jake Russo

Jami Hanreddy

Jason Fassl

Jason Waszak

Jennifer Vosters

Jon Kind

Julie Dubiner

Ken Williams

Kyla Vaughn

Laura Gordon

Linsey Falls

Maggie Monahan

Malkia Stampley

Marissa Abbott

Maya Danks

Meg Powers

Michael Weems

Michelle Lopez-Rios

Nancy Smith-Watson

Nicole Chandler

Patrick McGuire

Paul D'Amato

Raeleen McMillion

Rich Gillard

Ron Scott Fry

Sadie Lockhadt

Scott Hann

Sonia Goldberg

Sophronia Vowels

Susaan Jamshidi

Sydney Ray

#ENOUGH could not have been possible without the generosity of our Fractured Atlas campaign backers. Thank you, one and all.

Adam Belcoure

Amanda Hoffman

Amy Geyser

Andy & Jessie's X-Mas Gift

Andy Truschinski

Anne Basting

Annie Jurczyk

Anonymous

Arya Daire

Barbara Pitts McAdams

Bill Rausch

Brandy Kline

Brian Miracle

Caitlin McLeod

Catherine Cotey

Christian Fleming

Christina Puentes

Christopher Moore

Colette Walls

Craig Kingsley

Dani Stompor

Daniel Koester

David Cecsarini

David Rothrcok

Deondray Gossett

Diana Slickman

Diana Nelson

Elizabeth Biskobing

Elizabeth Warren

Erica Sorum

Erin Ogletree

Erin Wood

Frederick Kingsley

Gary Neal Johnson

Gene Behnke

George Brant

Guy Massey

Hallie Gordon

Hannah Todd

Hassan Al Rawas

Heather Hanson

Henry Wishcamper

Idris Goodwin

Isaac Schoepp

Jackson Doran

Jaclyn Loewenstein

Jamar Turner

James Stauffer

Jami Hanreddy

Jared Clarkin

Jeffrey Lieder

Jeffrey Thorn

Jerrell Henderson

Jessica Marking

Jessica Sarkes

Jessie Heesacker

Jill Anna Ponasik

Joe Dempsey

Joe Hanreddy

Joey Fitzpatrick

John Atwater

John Weidman

John J Ward

Josh Rosenberg

Judy Martel

Justinn Tanem

Karen Multer

Karyn Elliott

Kyla Vaughn

Laura Bessenecker

Lauren Gunderson

Lisa Steinkamp

Luke Erickson

Maryanne Yoshida

Matt Blasinski

Maureen Corrigan

Megan Kaminsky

Micah Sorum

Michael Wright

Michaela Petro

Mona Gracen

Nancy Smith-Watson

Neil Scharnick

Nicholas Harazin

Nicole Chandler

Patrick Holland

Patrick Schmitz

Raeleen McMillion

Randall Trumbull-Holper

Rita Crowley

Rob Wagner

Robert Westley

Roberta Inscho-Cox

Sally Stanton

Sammi Dittloff

Samuel Douglas

Sara Gosses

Scott Foley

Sean Graney

Sotirios Livaditis

Stacie Hauenstein

Steve Multer

Susan Pastin

Teresa Thorn

Theater RED

Thomas Strini

Tom Walls

Tommy Stevens

Travis Knight

Wayne T. Carr

Wendy Mapes

William Cain

William Lavonis